NEXT YEAR IN JERUSALEM

Dear Mr. Eisenberg —

Many thanks for your help via Steve Ebbin — I only hope this book is of some little effect on a big problem —

Bob Goldwater

Books by Robert Goldston

ROBERT GOLDSTON

NEXT YEAR IN JERUSALEM
A Short History of Zionism

An Atlantic Monthly Press Book
Little, Brown and Company   Boston   Toronto

FIRST EDITION

T03/78

LIBRARY OF CONGRESS CATALOGING IN PUBLICATION DATA

Goldston, Robert C
    Next year in Jerusalem.

    "An Atlantic Monthly Press book."
    Bibliography: p.
    Includes index.
    SUMMARY: Traces the history of Zionism from Biblical
times to the eventual establishment of a Zionist state
in Palestine.
    1. Zionism—History. 2. Jews—History. I. Title.
DS149.G5488   956.94′001   77-28057
ISBN 0-316-31958-9

ATLANTIC–LITTLE, BROWN BOOKS
ARE PUBLISHED BY
LITTLE, BROWN AND COMPANY
IN ASSOCIATION WITH
THE ATLANTIC MONTHLY PRESS

Published simultaneously in Canada
by Little, Brown & Company (Canada) Limited

PRINTED IN THE UNITED STATES OF AMERICA

For Paul Peyton Moffitt

The author wishes to express his thanks to The Dial Press for permission to quote a brief excerpt from *The Diaries of Theodore Herzl* by Marvin Lowenthal. Copyright © 1956 by The Dial Press. Reprinted by permission of the Dial Press. And to The Bobbs-Merrill Company for permission to quote from *Allenby of Armageddon* by Raymond Savage. Pages 56–57, 74–75, and 92–93 are taken from *The Jews in the Medieval World* by Jacob Rader Marcus and used with the agreement of the reprint publisher, Greenwood Press, Inc.

Contents

Prologue:

A Problem of History . . .

The voting began at 8:00 P.M. on November 10, 1975, in the spacious, modernistic hall of the United Nations General Assembly. The delegations of more than one hundred nations watched silently as the tally of those for and against the resolution flashed onto the large computer display behind the Secretary General's rostrum. Tension had been rising for hours — now the delegates could almost reach out and touch it. Blue-uniformed United Nations security guards were everywhere. Outside the Assembly Hall, on Manhattan's East Side, police barricades were going up, though no crowds had gathered — yet. Inside the hall, the visitors' galleries were half-empty; only carefully screened guests had been permitted to watch the proceedings.

The matter at issue was not one which would normally have engaged the passions of most delegates. They had only been asked to vote approval of a resolution submitted by the United Nations Social, Human and Cultural Committee calling for member states to join in a "Decade for the Elimination of Racism" all over the world. Surely a worthy, harmless, and neutral proposal. But to that resolution certain Arab nations had appended an amendment. This amendment read: "Zionism is a form of racism and racial discrimination."

The tension had arisen over the simple definition of a word: *Zionism.*

The delegates had already listened to a long, rambling discourse by Kuwait's representative, Fayez-Abdallah Sayegh, in which he was at some pains to insist that his opposition to Zionism was by no means based on a hatred of Jews. "We reject the equation between anti-Zionism and anti-Semitism," he declared. But the Israeli representative, Chaim Herzog, in an impassioned speech had likened the anti-Zionist resolution to Hitler's persecution of the Jews and, as he publicly tore his copy of the resolution to shreds at the rostrum, remarked, "The United Nations is on its way to becoming the world center of anti-Semitism."

By 8:30 the voting was over — and the resolution which stated that Zionism was a form of racism had been adopted by 75 votes to 35. Thirty-two nations abstained from voting; the delegations of three nations were absent. Daniel P. Moynihan, the fiery chief of the United States delegation, marched up to the rostrum and spoke with grim precision: "The United States rises to declare before the General Assembly of the United Nations and before the world that it does not acknowledge, it will not abide by, it will never acquiesce in this infamous act!" He then strode from the hall.

Later that night United Nations Secretary General Kurt Waldheim told reporters that the vote had revealed "a deep and bitter division among the membership." He deplored "the great passions on all sides." Most Arab and Third World African nations, as well as the Communist bloc, had voted to adopt the resolution; almost all the democracies, including the nations of western Europe, had voted against it. Not all the delegations even understood what they were doing. Delegate Radha Krishna Ramphul of Mauritius (who had voted for the resolution) later observed: "There was a lot of confusion. Many people voted without knowing what Zionism is. I am confused." A Latin American delegate, who refused to identify himself to reporters, admitted: "The Latin American countries that approved the anti-Zionist text . . . did so of course to butter up the Arabs whose oil and investment capital they want; but to a good measure, they acted just out of resentment of the Yankees."

Radha Krishna Ramphul may have been confused; but many thousands of Americans were not. The following day, November 11, tens of thousands of them gathered for a rally in midtown Manhattan to protest the UN resolution. New York Senator Jacob Javits said he viewed the anti-Zionist resolution with "moral loathing." President Gerald R. Ford sent a message to the rally in which he "deplored" the UN vote. Chaim Herzog told the crowd that when he heard which way the voting had gone, "I knew the thoughts of every Jew — whether he be in Elath or New York, in London or Buenos Aires, in Jerusalem or Mexico City, in São Paulo or Paris, in Moscow or Casablanca — were with me. I sensed the prayers of those languishing in the snow and windswept prison camps of Siberia, or the hell on earth that is the Jewish ghetto in Damascus."

In Washington, D.C., Secretary of State Henry Kissinger declared that the UN resolution showed "an example of the bloc voting, of the one-way morality, that has weakened public support of the United Nations in the United States." Both the Senate and the House of Representatives adopted unanimous resolutions calling upon the President to "reassess" United States participation in the United Nations — with the clear implication that many thought the time had come for the United States to withdraw from the world body. The prestigious *New York Times* called the anti-Zionist resolution "offensive, spiteful and futile — and stupid as well."

All this passion had been aroused over a single word: Zionism. What deep wellsprings of feeling had this word touched? Like other words such as *Freedom, Imperialism, Fascism,* and *Liberation, Zionism* evidently had the power to move men's hearts as well as their minds. Why? Like those other words, *Zionism* has a dictionary definition — but dictionary definitions do not explain the moral weight of words by which men live and die. Only history can do that; and the true meaning of Zionism is a problem of history. . . .

NEXT YEAR IN JERUSALEM

1

Slightly West of Eden

> Now the Lord said unto Abraham, Get thee out of thy
> country, and from thy kindred, and from thy father's house,
> unto the land that I will show thee: and I will make of thee
> a great nation.
>
> *Genesis 12:1*

And so Abraham, seventy-five years old but, like all the biblical Patriarchs, remarkably vigorous for his age, left the village
of Haran in southern Mesopotamia and headed west. Despite
the Lord's advice to travel light, Abraham brought along his
wife Sarah, his nephew Lot, and a host of wives, children,
concubines, servants, and hangers-on: in fact, an entire tribe.
Behind him he was leaving the Chaldean empire, with its great
stone cities of Babylon, Charchemish, and Ur (Abraham's father, Terah, had come from Ur) — ahead, beyond the western
deserts, lay the land of Canaan, which the Lord said should be
his: a promised land.

Abraham and his followers were used to traveling. Since
time immemorial they had been packing their tents and be-
longings on the backs of donkeys and camels and following
new horizons. They were nomadic shepherds, ever in search of
new and fertile pasture lands for their flocks of sheep and
goats. They were a fragment of the numerous Aramean tribes
who had migrated into Mesopotamia from the north around

the twentieth century B.C. Like all such migrating peoples, they
brought with them not only their flocks and their tents and
their household goods, but also their dreams, their poetry,
their tribal history: in the stories recited by old men around
the nightly campfires; in the songs sung by women at work; in
the tales handed down from generation to generation since the
beginning of time. And as they slowly wandered, across the
centuries they also adopted some of the traditions of the lands
through which they passed, until eventually it was hard to say
just where all the legends had come from — perhaps they were
universal.

Thus Abraham knew how God had created the universe in
six days, knew of the marvelous Garden of Eden, from which
mankind was now banished, knew of the builders of the
mighty tower of Babel and of how the Lord had punished
their pride, knew of the great flood which God had visited
upon the Earth and of how Noah and his family had built an
ark to escape the divine wrath. In fact, Abraham could trace
his lineage directly and very precisely back to Adam and Eve.
And if imagination sometimes decorated truth with fable, did
that make it any the less true? In the vast stillness of the desert
nights, with clouds of stars close enough to touch, the nomads
dreamed their dreams and sometimes heard the voice of their
God whispering to them from the rustling palm fronds. Their
God — for each tribe had a different divinity who helped or
hindered, led and judged, rewarded or punished just like the
tribal Patriarch, the "father-ruler" of his people. So when God
ordered Abraham to leave the land of the Chaldees and make
his way to Canaan, the aged Patriarch unhesitatingly obeyed.

But when Abraham and his people reached Canaan they
found the promised land already occupied — by Canaanites.
Now in the ancient tongue, *Canaan* meant "purple," and in
Greek the word for "purple" is *phoinix*, so that Canaan was

really ancient Phoenicia, and the Canaanites those daring sea adventurers and world traders, the Phoenicians. Later the descendants of Abraham referred to the people of this country as Pelishtim: "Philistines." Still later the Greek historian Herodotus wrote that word as "Palaistine" — and Palestine the land has been called to this day. In the days of Abraham, Palestine was still, indeed, a "garden of the Lord." Bounded on the west by the Mediterranean Sea, on the east by the desert, it stretched from the hills of Lebanon in the north to the gates of Egypt in the south. The land was divided in two by the River Jordan, which rises in Syria and flows south to the Dead Sea, some thirteen hundred feet below sea level, the deepest natural land depression on earth. Along its course the Jordan also feeds Lake Hueleh and the Sea of Galilee. South of the Dead Sea the valley of Araba stretches down to the Gulf of Aqaba on the Red Sea.

Palestine was part of the "fertile crescent," which joined Egypt and Mesopotamia, the principal caravan route between Asia and North Africa, and a pathway of conquest since before the dawn of history. Wealthy in trade, the Phoenicians had built the coastal cities of Tyre and Sidon as well as the inland hill city of Salem, which Abraham's people called "Jerushalayim." Blessed with rich soil, a mild climate, and abundant rain, its hillsides covered with vineyards and olive orchards, its pastures glistening green — no wonder the newly arrived desert nomads dubbed Palestine a "land of milk and honey."

Abraham's tribe settled in Canaan, as did other Aramean nomads — sometimes fighting the Canaanites, eventually blending with them. But they did not immediately adopt the city ways of the Phoenicians — for centuries they were to remain pastoral shepherds, grazing their flocks on the hills or the plains according to the season of the year. In times of drought they migrated south temporarily into Egypt, where with

Pharaoh's permission they might buy grain and rent pasture land to keep themselves alive.

And Abraham begat Isaac and Isaac begat Jacob and Jacob wrestled with an Angel of the Lord. It was a tough match, lasting all night, during which Jacob was permanently crippled — but the Angel finally gave in and allowed that Jacob could thenceforth call himself Israel. Now why did Jacob want so desperately to be called Israel? The word had only slight religious and no apparent political significance — it was merely a personal name. To be sure, it was a name of great antiquity even in Jacob's time. Modern archaeologists working in Syria have discovered a seal bearing the inscription "Israel, son of Rishzuni," which dates back to around 2700 B.C. But the name Jacob is equally old. The answer to this problem is one of the important keys to biblical interpretation.

It must be remembered that for thousands of years history was an oral art. The stories of the Pentateuch (the first five books of the Old Testament) were not compiled and actually written down until more than a thousand years after the events they record — our earliest fragments of Old Testament writings date from around 400 B.C. And in the oral tradition of history, the tale-teller often personified entire tribes and peoples by the names of their founders or greatest leaders or the names of towns or regions from which they came. Thus the name of Abraham's nephew Lot meant the tribes who inhabited the region called Lotun on the east bank of the Jordan; the word *Israel* referred to the entire tribe of a man called Israel and the word *Jacob* meant the people of Jacob, Abraham's grandson. So Jacob's wrestling match with the Angel of God may very well have been the poetic record of the merging (perhaps by conquest) of the tribes of Israel and Jacob.

How good a guide is the Pentateuch to the real history of the Jewish people? It was never intended to be a history; it was intended to be the record of God's interventions in history. More than that, it is an entire literature of a people. Yet through all the wonders and marvels, the poetry and fable of the Old Testament, the broad outlines of history may be discerned. And modern research and archaeology gives substantial support to those outlines.

So when we read of Jacob's son Joseph being sold into slavery in Egypt, we are learning of the misfortune which befell an entire tribe of Israelites. And Egyptian history — inscribed on tablets and the walls of tombs — records more than a few instances of shepherd tribes entering the land as slaves captured in battle. Nor is there any reason to doubt the biblical story that during a time of drought and famine in Palestine, other Israelite tribes (personified in the Old Testament as other sons of Jacob) also took refuge in Egypt. Once there they were apparently forced into the downtrodden and despised social class called Habiri, or "Hebrews" — day laborers who were not quite slaves. There they were to remain until Moses led them out of Egypt and back to the promised land.

The sufferings of the Israelite slaves in Egypt must have been cruel. Real slavery on the scale practiced in ancient Egypt was unknown to the shepherd tribes. Although the Patriarchs had had "bondsmen" and "bondswomen," these were few and almost always employed in the household. Caring for flocks of sheep and goats did not require great manpower; and a nomadic existence, with the tribes constantly on the move between pasture lands, would have afforded too many opportunities for slaves to escape. Then, too, the shepherd economy was by no means rich enough to support slaves — it was barely able to support the families of the tribe.

But Egypt, which had enjoyed a settled agricultural life for thousands of years before the coming of the Israelites, had developed into a real slave state. The caste of warriors and priests, who ruled the land and from whose ranks emerged the semidivine Pharaohs, had need of slaves — to develop the irrigation projects which brought the life-giving waters of the Nile to farmlands many miles from its banks; to build the great cities which were both central marketplaces and fortresses for the ruling classes. In ancient times there was no other way these things could be done — manpower was the only power available. Just as modern economies depend on electric and internal-combustion energy, so the economies of the ancient empires depended upon human energy. And since men would not willingly exhaust their lives in the creation of wealth which was not theirs, slavery — forced labor — came into existence.

Historians are agreed that the emergence of both the Israelite religion and the Israelite nation (as opposed to a scattering of tribes) really begins with the advent of Moses and the Exodus of the mingled Israelites and Hebrews from Egypt. Moses, the greatest figure of Jewish history (the name means "he who draws forth" or "liberates") may be said to have founded three of the world's great religions: Judaism, Christianity, and Mohammedanism, since all three trace their roots back to him. His biblical career was embellished with legends which were already ancient in his own time; it became the prototype legend for the lives of later religious founders.

According to the Old Testament, Moses was born of the lowly caste of Hebrews, adopted by Pharaoh's daughter and raised an Egyptian prince. As a young man, however, he tried to protect his Hebrew brethren from their cruel Egyptian taskmasters. For slaying an Egyptian overseer he was driven from Egypt and he took refuge in the eastern desert — northern Arabia. There he first heard the Voice of God: "I am the God of thy father, the God of Abraham, the God of Isaac, and the God of Jacob." This identification was necessary because the Israelite tribes and the Hebrews worshipped more than a few gods. But the God who spoke to Moses was the God of the Jacobite tribes, called Yah or Yahu or Yahweh — the God we know as Jehovah. And Jehovah commanded Moses to return to Egypt and lead His people out of bondage and back to Canaan. When Moses balked at such a tremendous task, Jehovah promised His aid.

That aid took awesome forms: the visitation of terrible plagues upon the Egyptians, the parting of the Red Sea to allow the Israelites to cross, the drowning of Pharaoh and his entire army — all of which are almost certainly later embellishments of the Moses story. For Egyptian history, which is generally quite detailed and reasonably accurate, remains utterly silent about these tremendous events. Modern scholars have speculated that the Jacobite tribes probably entered Egypt around 1300 B.C. — during the reign of Pharaoh Ikhnaton (who was the only Pharaoh to worship *one* god — the sun), that Moses was born around 1290 B.C. and that the Exodus took place around 1230 B.C.

Having miraculously escaped their Egyptian pursuers, the Israelites and Hebrews followed Moses through the "wilderness" (the Sinai desert) to Mount Horeb — a place never satisfactorily identified. There the tribes waited while Moses climbed the mountain alone, communed with God, and then returned with the Ten Commandments — commandments he claimed Jehovah Himself had inscribed with a fiery finger upon stone tablets. These commandments contained many of the ancient beliefs and laws of both the Israelites and the Hebrews (thus helping to unify Moses' followers), as well as something startlingly new. This was the First Commandment: "The Lord thy God is a jealous God and thou shalt have no other gods before Him." The observance of this commandment to worship but one God was to set the Israelites apart from all the peoples of the ancient world. It at once elevated the tribal God, Jehovah, to supremity, omnipotence, and, by implication, placed Him beyond the tribal limits — made of Him a cosmic, universal spirit. This belief, and the rules of behavior incorporated in the other commandments, furnished the ethical basis of all future western religions. And the Ten Commandments became, in a sense, the "Constitution" of the landless, stateless Jewish nation, as they wandered through the desert. Those individuals, tribes, and peoples who agreed to observe these commandments (much extended and embellished with other laws, rituals, and observances) would be accepted as Jews.

Such a central code of beliefs was essential to the survival of the Israelites as a nation in the absence of a national home or state. Such a means of confirming nationality is not unknown to other peoples, in more recent times. Thus, while a Frenchman is "French" simply by birth, an Englishman "English," an American confirms his nationality through allegiance to certain basic laws and ideals embodied in the Constitution of the United States and the Declaration of Independence. This is the natural result of our creation of a multinational society, which has expanded through large-scale immigration from other lands. It marks the distinction between citizenship as a positive function and the accident of nationality by birth. The idea that a nation might be defined by its beliefs and ideals as well as, or even apart from, its national territory — an idea which animates not only American but also various Communist societies — was born in the wilderness outside Canaan.

The tablets which Moses brought down from the mountain were more than a list of commandments. They also represented a covenant (treaty) between the Israelites and God. In essence the treaty promised that so long as the Jews strictly observed all of God's commandments, laws, and rituals, God would protect them and advance their interests. And just as the United States Constitution is enshrined in an airtight, highly protected environment in Washington, D.C., so the Tablets of the Law were guarded and enshrined in a wooden ark, which was known as the Ark of the Covenant and which would accompany the Israelite nation wherever it wandered.

Now the Lord had promised Moses to lead His people back to Canaan. But Moses died without setting eyes on the promised land. It was Joshua, the son of Nun, one of Moses' servants, who led the Israelites back into Palestine. And once again the nomads had to fight their way in, as they had centuries earlier under Abraham. The legend of Joshua bringing down the walls of the city of Jericho with a blast on his ram's horn is the prototype fable of a period of conquest.

When the Israelites reentered Canaan (around 1100 B.C.), it was a land of numerous independent city-states, constantly at war with each other, acknowledging the distant overlordship of the Egyptian Pharaohs. Lacking siege equipment, the nomads had great difficulty in conquering the Phoenician cities; for many decades they lived in the hills and waged a prolonged guerrilla warfare against the fortified towns. Eventually they conquered all of Palestine west of the Jordan — though the most important cities, the coastal plain, and control of the vital trade routes remained in Phoenician hands. Of course this conquest took many years — and, during it, as new areas came under Israelite control, the various tribes composing the Israelite nation were granted lands to hold — until all twelve tribes had been accommodated. The fighting, as described in the Old Testament books of Joshua and Judges, was fierce and often accompanied by wholesale massacre of the losers. But the Israelites were convinced not only that they were righteously repossessing the land of their forefathers, but also that they were fulfilling the will of God. And, since the time of Moses, that God was not simply a tribal divinity, but the One True God of the universe — which meant that the gods of the enemy were no more than heathen idols. It is fair to assume that the spirit of the Israelite conquest of Palestine was akin to the spirit that animated the Mohammedan conquest of North Africa and Spain, the Crusaders' conquest of the Holy Land, and the Catholic-Protestant wars of sixteenth- and seventeenth-century Europe. Religious wars are always the cruelest — and the wars described in Joshua were no different.

But to apologize for conquest by saying it is God's will always raises the embarrassing question of how to explain defeat. If God led Israel, how could the Israelites lose battles (as they often did) to their enemies? The answer they gave was the same as that given by all later religious warriors: they suffered defeat because they had turned away from God. By breaking God's commandments they were also breaking God's covenant, and would suffer dire punishment for it. This theme of the Israelites' falling away from God, undergoing calamity as a result and then finally being led back to the true faith became central to the Jewish consciousness.

After Joshua, during the long bloody wars of the conquest of Palestine, the Israelites were ruled by "Judges." These were usually military leaders, whose authority was based, not on inherited titles, but on a special relationship with God. Their power was generally restricted to small areas of Palestine and individual tribes. These were the days of the great general, Gideon, and the mighty warrior, Samson. They were also, more importantly, the centuries during which the Israelite nomads were gradually changing from a shepherding to a settled agricultural economy in Palestine. But the wars with the Philistines (Phoenicians) went on — until the Hebrew tribes

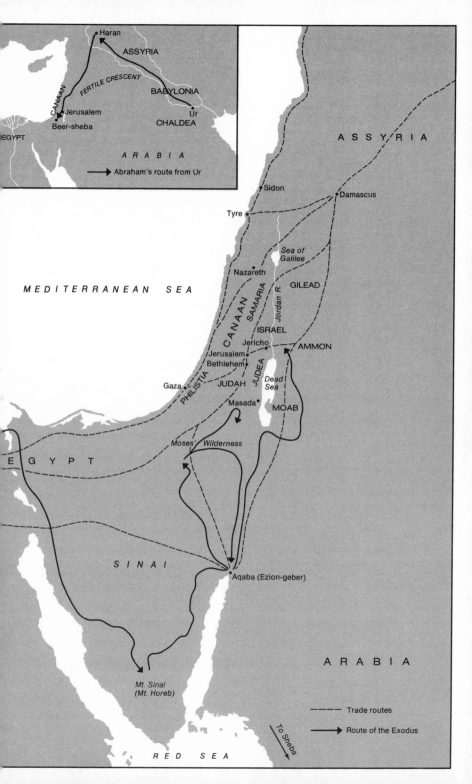

Haran

ASSYRIA

FERTILE CRESCENT

BABYLONIA

CANAAN

Jerusalem

Beer-sheba

Ur

CHALDEA

EGYPT

ARABIA

→ Abraham's route from Ur

ASSYRIA

MEDITERRANEAN SEA

Sidon

Damascus

Tyre

Sea of Galilee

Nazareth

GILEAD

Jordan R.

SAMARIA

CANAAN

ISRAEL

Jericho

AMMON

Jerusalem

Bethlehem

JUDEA

Gaza

PHILISTIA

JUDAH

Dead Sea

Masada

MOAB

Moses' Wilderness

EGYPT

SINAI

Aqaba (Ezion-geber)

ARABIA

To Sheba

Mt. Sinai (Mt. Horeb)

RED SEA

- - - Trade routes

→ Route of the Exodus

suffered a disastrous defeat at Shiloh and even lost the sacred
Ark of the Covenant to their enemies.

The Ark, after bringing plagues and all sorts of misfortunes
to the Phoenicians, was soon returned by them to its rightful
owners, who had been led back into the paths of righteousness
by the last and greatest of all the Judges, Samuel. It was Samuel who more firmly united the Hebrew tribes and, at their
request (and against his better judgment), appointed a hereditary king to rule over them "like all the nations." This event
— a revolution in Hebrew life — was the natural result of the
transformation of tribes of nomadic shepherds into a nation of
settled farmers and peasants. It was even a requirement of that
transformation. For an agricultural economy depends above
all else on security and continuity — the security of irrigation
projects and trade routes, the security of central marketplaces,
the security of permanent protection against marauding
bands — and a continuity of administration of taxes and other
complexities of settled national life.

All of these things Saul, David, Solomon, and a long line of
kings attempted to provide for the Hebrews. But the nomadic
heritage of freedom persisted under the monarchy. For it soon
developed that the crown would not be hereditary but would
descend to whoever the people themselves felt deserved it. If a
king proved himself corrupt, tyrannical, or just plain stupid,
it proved that he had fallen from God's grace — and his (often
bloody) overthrow was perfectly justified. Far from becoming
semidivine gods themselves (like almost all kings and em-
perors of the ancient world, from Pharaoh to Caesar), the
kings of the Hebrews were understood to be no more than
servants of God's will and of His chosen people — and woe to
the king who misbehaved.

The wars against the Phoenicians were pursued by Saul and,
later, David with some success. It was David who conquered

the Phoenician city of Jerusalem, brought the Ark of the Covenant there, and attempted to build a temple to house it. But he never accomplished this task; the Ark continued to be sheltered in a simple nomadic tent, as it always had been. It was left to Solomon, David's successor, to build a magnificent temple in Jerusalem to house the "Holy of Holies."

So Jerusalem, and the hill called Zion upon which the city stood, became not only a national capital but also a national shrine. And the Temple priests, who charged pilgrims and other worshippers for their services in preparing sacrifices of lambs to Jehovah, waxed rich and influential. Solomon himself became legendary for his wisdom, but the proverbs attributed to him, like the gorgeous Psalms of David, are the work of many different writers over the course of many centuries.

The magnificence of Solomon's works — the Temple, the palaces, the great walls of Jerusalem — could not be realized without a heavy increase in taxes. This led to the growth of opposition — especially among the northern Hebrew tribes, who resented not only the tax collectors but also the beginnings of a class-bound social structure in place of their formerly democratic society. Some years after Solomon's death (in 931 B.C.) the northern tribes rebelled against his heir, Rehoboam, and seceded from the kingdom. They established a kingdom of their own, which they called Israel — and they returned to earlier political traditions. Thus the kings of Israel were chosen, as they had been during the time of Judges, by the people, on the basis of proven ability, and confirmed by religious leaders.

The southern Hebrew tribes remained loyal to Solomon's heirs and the idea of hereditary kingship. They established the kingdom of Judah, which included Jerusalem. The wars between the Hebrews and their neighbors were now complicated by wars between Israel and Judah.

Of course none of the kingdoms or city-states of Palestine —
neither Israelite, Judean, nor Phoenician — was ever for very
long free in any absolute sense. Palestine was much too important a trade route, much too inviting a pathway of conquest, to
enjoy the neglect of great neighboring empires. Unless those
empires were weakened by outside attack or internal dissen-
sion, one or another of them generally claimed overlordship in
Canaan. The Egyptians, the Chaldeans, the Babylonians, the
Assyrians — all took tribute from the petty kings in Palestine
when they could. The chaos of conflict in Palestine was always
complicated further by the constant game of playing off the
great empires against each other, whenever that was possible,
and appeasing them when it was not.

The game ended disastrously for the kingdom of Israel early
in the eighth century B.C. The Assyrian king, Shalmaneser
V, who claimed overlordship of Israel, found out that the Israelite king, Hoshea, was plotting with the Egyptians against
Assyria. He had Hoshea imprisoned and occupied the kingdom. The city of Samaria held out for a while but was finally
captured by Shalmaneser's successor, King Sargon II, in 721
B.C. Sargon deported most of the Israelites to other areas of his
empire, where they disappeared from history. He then resettled the kingdom of Israel with colonists from Babylon. But
these colonists fared badly — they were stricken by famines
and plagues and, finally, an invasion of lions. The Assyrians
were told by their Israelite neighbors that this was because the
new inhabitants did not know the "law of the god of the land."
They hastily summoned back one of the deported Israelite
priests and ordered him to teach the new settlers the ways of
Jehovah. In this way Samaria (as the land was now called) became an Assyrian province with a mixed population, which
worshipped Jehovah and felt itself bound by the Law of
Moses. But the Samaritans retained a feeling of national and

religious separateness which was not disposed to yield to any claims later made by Jerusalem.

The southern kingdom of Judah (from which derives the word *Jew*, meaning inhabitant or descendant of Judah) managed to escape the harsher consequences of Assyrian conquest by accepting the invaders as overlords. But when the power of Assyria began to crumble under the assaults of the Medes (and the subsequent revolt of the Babylonians) in the seventh century B.C., the Judean kings were once again forced into the risky game of international power politics. They hoped for protection against the resurgent Babylonians by making an alliance with Egypt. They guessed wrong and, in 586 B.C., the Babylonian king, Nebuchadnezzar II, destroyed the kingdom of Judah, wrecked much of Jerusalem, tore down the Temple built by Solomon (no man has seen the Ark of the Covenant since that time), and carried away as captives the rich and influential among the Judeans — perhaps twenty percent of the entire population.

Thus began the Babylonian Exile and, with it, some of the most important aspects of modern Judaism. It was in Babylon, where the Jews longed for their return to the holy city built on the hill of Zion, that the first expression of "Zionism" was uttered, in a psalm, with the words "If I forget thee, O Jerusalem, let my right hand forget her cunning." And it was in Babylon that the exiled Jews, far from their destroyed temple and their holy shrines, discovered that they had a religious heritage which needed neither temples nor shrines. They returned to the old nomadic vision of their relationship with God.

In Babylon it became customary for pious Jews to gather regularly in groups in order to recite the sacred texts together, to pray, and to listen to the most learned men among them interpret religious doctrine. Even after they returned to Palestine, this regular assembly continued as a practice, both in areas distant from the rebuilt Temple in Jerusalem and in Babylon, where a large segment of the Jewish community remained permanently settled. The Greeks called these assemblies synagogues — a term which only much later came to refer to the building in which such meetings took place. The synagogue was the most important bridge between ancient and modern Judaism and the model chosen by Paul for the earliest Christian churches.

An essential element of the synagogue was the learned man who interpreted the ancient texts, taught the congregation, and led it — the prototype of the modern rabbi. But while the rabbi fulfilled certain priestly functions, he was not a priest — and the differences were profound. A priest of the Temple was a member of an hereditary class, born into his title. The Temple priests had always been an arm of the government, allies and functionaries of the ruling classes. But the rabbi was a man freely chosen by his congregation simply on the basis of his learning and wisdom — and could be dismissed by them. These early rabbis are sometimes referred to as "scribes" in the New Testament — later as leaders of the Pharisees.

The end of the Babylonian Exile came with the end of the Babylonian kingdom, which was destroyed by the Persians under Cyrus in 539 B.C. Cyrus, while claiming overlordship in Palestine, allowed the exiled Jews to return to Jerusalem. There they soon built a new Temple and appointed priests to serve in it. But the synagogue tradition (though it was opposed by the priests of the Temple) was too strong to die. It spread through Palestine and to Jewish communities in Egypt and Persia as well.

Cyrus was apparently a tolerant monarch — but some of his successors were not. They tried to enforce various forms of idol worship in their realms (no doubt as a means of unifying it)

but soon found that the Jews, unlike any of their other subjects, would worship no other God than Jehovah. At a time
when religion was one of the pillars of the state, refusal to
recognize the imperial cult amounted to high treason — and
the Jews were punished accordingly. But for the Jews, their
religion was their national identity — just as it had been when
they were landless nomads — and the more it was threatened,
the fiercer became Jewish determination to preserve it.

The Persian Empire succumbed, early in the fourth century
B.C., to the Greeks, led by Alexander the Great, who established an empire of his own. But this did not immediately
affect the Jews, who were simply forced to exchange Persian
for Greek rule. Indeed, Greek influence in Palestine had been
great long before the conquests of Alexander. Greek merchants, artists, craftsmen, and such writers as Herodotus and
Xenophon traveled extensively throughout the Mideast,
spreading Greek culture wherever they went. Greek words
crept into Hebrew, and Greek concepts into the Jewish consciousness. The philosophical discourse of the Book of Job, for
example, is thought to reflect Greek influence.

Upon Alexander's death in 323 B.C., his empire broke up
into smaller kingdoms ruled by his Greek successors. Several of
these quarreled over domination of Palestine. For a while the
Ptolemies (Greek kings of Egypt) ruled the area; later it fell
under the sway of the Seleucid (Greek-Syrian) Empire. So
prolonged and destructive was the fighting (much of which
took place in Palestine) that thousands of Jews migrated to
Egypt — particularly to the new city of Alexandria, which
granted full citizenship to all foreigners. Only in 200 B.C.
when the Seleucid king, Antiochus III, finally conquered the
region, did life in Palestine become peaceful again.

Peaceful — but increasingly burdensome. For the Seleucid
kings were almost always at war; if not with the Egyptians,

then with the Persians or the Romans. And that meant conscription in Palestine for the Seleucid army, and heavier taxa-
tion for the Seleucid treasury. Furthermore, while the
Seleucids permitted the Jews their traditional religion and
forms of worship, they reserved the right to appoint the High
Priest of the Temple in Jerusalem, and made the priests of the
Temple responsible for tax collection. When, in the year 175
B.C., Antiochus IV ascended the Seleucid throne and began to
withdraw the privileges previously enjoyed by Jews — including the right to worship God in their own way, Jewish tempers
boiled over. When Antiochus appointed one Menelaus High
Priest in Jerusalem, heathen "abominations" began to be
practiced in the Temple itself — and armed rebellion began.

This ushered in a generation of fighting known as the Maccabean War — so named because the Jewish leaders of the
struggle, the five sons of Mattathias, adopted that word (it
meant "hammer") as their guerrilla code name. They waged a
hit-and-run campaign against the Seleucid forces in Palestine
until, in 164 B.C., they finally conquered Jerusalem. Their
victory owed much to the fact that the Seleucid Empire was
already decaying from within and crumbling under attack by
Asiatic tribes without. It also owed much to the fact that the
Maccabeans had signed a treaty of friendship and alliance with
Rome. For while the Romans sent no military help to the
Maccabeans, their powerful legions made warlike noises on the
Seleucid borders, thereby tying down strong Seleucid forces.
The Maccabean kings (they founded a royal dynasty of their
own once the Seleucids had been driven out) made the
Roman alliance a cornerstone of their foreign policy.

Under the Maccabean kings the borders of the Jewish state
in Palestine expanded to include almost all the formerly
Phoenician coastline and a large area on the east bank of the
River Jordan. But these Maccabean conquests brought in their

wake the usual oppressions: high taxes, military conscription, the hiring of foreign mercenaries (who inspired loathing among the people), and the militarization of the nation. Furthermore, the later Maccabean kings discarded their religious orthodoxy as they discarded their martial virtues. They grew sophisticated and became so Hellenized (that is, so influenced by Greek ways) that they even wrote their names in Greek and fell further and further away from the ancient Laws of Moses. Pious Jews — both the Sadducees, who followed the temple traditions of the priests, and the Pharisees, who followed the synagogue tradition — grew to hate this increasingly paganized dynasty.

The conflict between religious Jews and their Maccabean rulers reached its climax during the reign of Jonathan (103–76 B.C.), who styled himself, in the Greek fashion, Alexander Jannaeus. Jonathan, or Jannaeus, waged a number of generally unsuccessful wars. Between campaigns he officiated, as had his Maccabean predecessors, as High Priest of the Temple. The idea that a military man should hold this office was utterly repugnant to most Jews — and they expressed their displeasure by bombarding the king with lemons when he presided over the Feast of Tabernacles in the Temple. Jannaeus responded by setting his Asiatic mercenary troops on his own people, killing more than six thousand of them. The resulting civil war lasted six years, and in the end the rebels lost.

To all of this the silent spectator was Rome. The policy of the Roman Senate was one of cautious expansion; if possible they preferred to "divide and conquer" rather than indulge in wasteful fighting. Thus Rome maintained its alliance with the Jews only as a means of weakening the Seleucid Empire. Later, when that empire fell without a struggle to the Roman general Pompey, Jewish independence no longer served a useful purpose to Rome. A family quarrel among the Maccabean heirs of

Jannaeus provided a pretext for Pompey to send his legions
into Palestine and, in 63 B.C., both the Maccabean dynasty and
the Jewish state lost their freedom. Palestine was divided into
a number of small Roman provinces and placed under the
authority of a Roman governor, or Procurator. The descendants of the Maccabeans were permitted to continue in
office as High Priests of the Temple and later, some were even
permitted to call themselves kings — but real authority in
Palestine was henceforth exercised by Rome; Jewish "kings,"
"ethnarchs," "tetrarchs," and "dynasts" were no more than
Roman puppets. Manipulated as glorified tax collectors by the
Romans, these last "independent" rulers of Judea (as the
Romans named their new province) were loathed by the Jewish people. This was especially true after 37 B.C., when the last
Maccabean king (who was, for all his faults, at least Jewish)
was murdered and replaced by a new dynasty founded by a
friend of Augustus Caesar, the self-styled Herod the Great,
who was only half-Jewish by birth and all Roman by inclina-
tion.

Like all the empires of antiquity, Rome was a slave state. It
was slave power that worked the silver and lead mines of
Greece, slave power that rowed Roman trade galleys across the
Mediterranean, slave power that worked her vast agricultural
plantations, equipped her invincible legions, and built the
roads which knit her vast empire together. But slave power
was perhaps the most expensive energy source of all. It was self-
consuming, since the slave's brutal life was short. The need for
more and more slaves to satisfy the growing population was
never-ending. The supply could be increased only through
conquest — which meant an ever-larger military establishment
and ever-higher taxes and conscriptions. Militarism had already changed the Roman Republic into a dictatorship by the
time of Julius Caesar — after the civil wars which followed his

assassination it made that dictatorship hereditary under Augustus.

It was, of course, to Roman advantage that peace reign within the empire. For that reason, as long as taxes were promptly paid, slaves provided, and, when necessary, military conscription enforced, Roman governors interfered as little as possible in the lives of their subject peoples. All religions were recognized, but in turn the governors expected conquered peoples to recognize the Roman religion, which had degenerated into a form of emperor-worship with the Caesars assuming divinity. This created no special problems anywhere within the pagan empire — except in Palestine. There Roman beliefs collided with Judaism, a religion which was both the essence of a nationality and universalist in its claims. No Jew could obey all the laws of Rome without breaking the Laws of Moses; no Jew could recognize the divinity of Caesar and remain a Jew. To be a Jew in the Roman Empire was to be automatically guilty of high treason. Yet the Romans could afford to overlook even that provided their more worldly requirements were met.

Those requirements weighed ever more heavily on Palestine. The increasing taxes, the cruelty of the puppet regimes of Herod and his successors, the ever-more-frequent conscription of able-bodied men for the Roman armies, the outrage of the slave trade — all of these things maddened the Jews. But the power of Imperial Rome seemed unassailable.

While Jewish opinion was united in its detestation of Rome, it differed in emphasis. The Sadducees, the party of the Temple priests, interested only in the strictest observance of the letter of the Mosaic Law, was prepared to appease the Romans so long as their rights and privileges were protected. The Pharisees, inheritors of the synagogue traditions of the Exile, sought to reanimate Jewish national consciousness by new interpretations of the Law and a return to the purity of the old nomadic vision. The Zealots placed their emphasis on resistance to Rome in this world — they were the party of fanatical Jewish nationalism. The Essenes, perhaps in despair of righting the wrongs of a chaotic society, had long since retreated into a kind of monasticism in their strongholds near the Dead Sea. Jewish suffering gave rise to new religious sects which sought other ways to combat, or at least endure, the Roman tyranny. Jesus of Nazareth was the leader of one such group. And in the face of their own impotence against Roman power, Jews of all parties prayed for divine intervention — the coming of a Messiah to unite them against their oppressors — and the restoration of Jewish independence as it had been known in the days of David and Solomon.

Over all of this the Roman Procurators kept a close watch. Judea gained the reputation of being the most troublesome region in the entire empire. But rebellion in Palestine could not be tolerated — the province was much too vital strategically. Its loss could shake the Roman hold on Egypt and Syria and weaken the eastern boundaries of the empire. For this reason, potential leaders of Jewish uprisings were often deported to Rome, sold into slavery, or, as in the case of Jesus, executed. But Jewish nationalism refused to die. Riots, assassinations of Roman officials, and the ravages of marauding bands of guerrillas multiplied.

The spark which ignited nationwide rebellion came in A.D. 66, when the Emperor Nero demanded that Eleazar, High Priest of the Temple in Jerusalem, publicly sacrifice to the emperor as a god. Eleazar refused, and Zealots rose against Roman garrisons throughout Judea. The rebel cause, though looked upon with some apprehension by Sadducees and Pharisees (Christians either fled the country or maintained neutrality), soon swept the land. The Zealots captured Jerusalem and defeated a Roman legion sent against them.

The Roman response was not long in arriving. Nero's general in the area, Vespasian, a very capable commander, recaptured Galilee in A.D. 67. By the summer of A.D. 69, after bitter and costly fighting, Vespasian had subjugated most of the country. When, in that same year, Vespasian departed for Rome to assume the title of Emperor, he left his son Titus behind with orders to continue the fight. Titus took Jerusalem in A.D. 70 after a prolonged siege. The holy city and the Temple were both razed to the ground and, although the Zealot fortress of Masada near the Dead Sea held out for another three years, the rebellion was effectively at an end.

But not Jewish nationalism, nor Jewish adherence to the Laws of Moses. For when, some sixty years later, the Emperor Hadrian decided to rebuild Jerusalem as a Roman city and to construct a temple to the god Jupiter on Mount Zion, where once the Temple had stood, the Jews, led by one Simon "Bar Kochba" ("son of the star") rebelled yet again against the might of Rome. The fighting, furious as usual, lasted for three years until, in A.D. 135, the last Jewish stronghold fell.

Bar Kochba's rebellion proved to be the last straw for Rome. Romans had ruled Palestine for two centuries now and what had they to show for it? Only riots, rebellions, the blood of their subjects, and the deaths of thousands of good legionaries. Worst of all, a subversive influence was spreading throughout the empire. The Romans could tolerate the Jewish religion, but not the Jewish morality that was inseparable from that religion. Through the Jews scattered all over the empire, but especially through one of their abominable sects, the so-called Christians, wrongheaded ideas about national freedom, personal liberty, the evils of slavery, and militarism

— ideas that threatened the very foundations of the Roman state — were creeping into men's minds.

It was enough and more than enough. Rome formally put an end to all vestiges of Judean independence, parceling out sections of Palestine to other provinces. Jerusalem was plowed under and rebuilt as the Roman city Aelia Capitolina, dedicated to the god Jupiter. No Jew, under pain of death, was permitted to enter this city or even its immediate environs. Many thousands of Jews were deported, thousands of others sold into slavery. Jewish religious practices such as circumcision, the keeping of the Sabbath, and the teaching of the Law were forbidden — as was the ordination of priests. Those who resisted these edicts were put to death. It was Rome's "final solution to the Jewish problem."

And so, after thousands of years, the Jewish national state ceased to exist. The children of Abraham, whom the Lord had so long ago led forth from Ur of the Chaldees into the promised land of Canaan, were once again to become nomads — wanderers over the face of the earth.

Haggada:

The Fall of Masada

The night before the Jewish fortress of Masada fell to the Romans in A.D. 72, the priest Eleazar ben Yair made a speech to the surviving defenders, urging them to take their own lives as well as the lives of their women and children rather than submit to Roman slavery. His words have come down to us through the works of the historian Flavius Josephus, a renegade Jew in the employ of Rome:

"Since we long ago, my generous friends, resolved never to be servants of the Romans, nor to any other than to God Himself . . . the time is now come that obliges us to make that resolution true in practice. . . .

"We were the very first that revolted from them [the Romans], and we are the last that fight against them; and I cannot but esteem it as a favour that God hath granted us that it is still in our power to die bravely, and in a state of freedom.

"And as for those that are already dead in the war, it is reasonable that we should esteem them blessed, for they are dead in defending, and not in betraying their liberty; but as to the multitude of those who are now under the Romans, who would not pity their condition? And who would not make haste to die, before he would share the same miseries with them?

". . . Let us pity ourselves, our children, and our wives, while it is in our power to show pity to them; for we are born to die, as well as those were whom we have begotten: nor is it in the power of the most happy of our race to avoid it. But for abuses and slavery . . . these are not such evils as are natural and necessary among men . . .

"But certainly our hands are still at liberty, and have a sword in them; let them be subservient to us in our glorious design; let us die before we become slaves under our enemies, and let us go out of the world, together with our children and our wives, in a state of freedom."

And so they did. Only two old women and five children, who had hidden themselves away in one of the water cisterns, survived to tell the tale to the stunned Roman soldiers when they entered upon that scene of death the next morning.

2

The State Becomes a Memory

> Ask, is it well, O Thou consumed in fire
> With those who mourn for Thee. . . .
> MEIR OF ROTHENBURG

Now it happened during the Roman siege of Jerusalem in A.D. 70 that a rabbi named Johanan ben Zakkai, in order to escape the approaching massacre, pretended to be dead and had himself smuggled out of the doomed city in a coffin. Once safely beyond the Roman lines, the rabbi resurrected himself and gained an audience with Titus (Vespasian's son), the commander of the besieging legions. Johanan asked Titus to allow him to make his way to the town of Jabneh on the Mediterranean coast near Jaffa, where he wished to found a school for the study of Torah, the sacred Laws of Moses. Reflecting, no doubt, that the more Jews devoted to scholarship, the fewer he would have to fight, Titus agreed. He granted jurisdiction over Jabneh and over the spiritual, if not the temporal, life of Palestine to Johanan, who, like his successors, was allowed to style himself "Patriarch."

It was at Jabneh, shortly thereafter, that Johanan heard of the fall of Jerusalem and the destruction of the Temple. The aged rabbi rent his garments but consoled his weeping fol-

lowers with the thought that the Jews possessed a substitute for
the Temple in their synagogues. For Johanan was a Pharisee
and inherited the traditions of the Babylonian Exile. The
school he founded devoted itself, after the Pharisaical custom,
to the study, discussion, and interpretation of holy scripture
and Jewish law. Not that the scholars of Jabneh easily gave up
hope of Jewish national independence (one of them, the
Rabbi Akiba ben Joseph, was instrumental in organizing the
disastrous Bar Kochba Rebellion in A.D. 133), but because of
the Roman oppression their efforts were centered upon the
preservation of Jewish religious beliefs and culture as the only
possible expression of Jewish nationalism. Their great work of
religious and legal interpretation was called the Mishnah and
was passed on from generation to generation orally. It was not
until after Bar Kochba's uprising, when the Romans seemed
intent upon the utter destruction not only of Jewish nationality but also of Judaism itself, that the Mishnah was committed
to writing. This was done around the year A.D. 200. To be
sure, the Mishnah did not thereupon become a finished work;
for centuries to come learned scholars and rabbis would add
their comments to its text.

Perhaps the most important contributions to the Mishnah
were made not in Palestine, but far from the immediate reach
of the Romans — in Mesopotamia; once the Babylonian, now
the Persian, Empire. Many Jews, it will be recalled, had remained in Babylon after the days of the Exile; many thousands
more joined them over the centuries of warfare and rebellion
that turned Palestine into a desert. Although the Jews of Babylon suffered their share of persecution and massacre as various
conquerors came and went, by and large they prospered. By
the time the Romans were plowing under the walls of Jerusalem, the Jews of Babylon numbered hundreds of thousands.
They had their own schools, synagogues, and civil courts, and

were allowed to govern their own affairs under the leadership of "exilarchs" (literally, "rulers of the exile").

The Mishnah, with its laws and commentaries, was known as the Halakha (or "way of walking," "manner of living") — but there was also the Haggada (or "telling"), which included everything that was not Halakha: history, folklore, medicine, biography, ethics, sciences, logic, memoirs, and a vast mass of legends. All of this huge, diverse mass — Halakha and Haggada together — was called the Talmud (the "teaching") and when, around A.D. 450, it seemed that renewed Persian persecution would soon wipe out the synagogues of Mesopotamia as the Romans had obliterated those of Palestine, the Talmud was written down in its entirety.

What the Pharisees and their descendants in Palestine and Mesopotamia had accomplished was the creation of a sort of portable foundation for a nation-in-exile. They had compiled not only the religious beliefs and laws, but also the entire history, art, myth, and wisdom of a people — its very way of life. Wherever Jews might wander, no matter how terrible their sufferings, the Talmud provided another world into which they could escape — a homeland they could carry with them while their own land was lost. They were very truly called "The People of the Book."

The scattering of Jews throughout the ancient world had begun long before the Romans first came to Palestine. Jewish merchants and sea traders (no doubt learning from their neighbors the Phoenicians) had traveled to every part of the Mediterranean. Jewish communities were to be found in Egypt, Carthage, Greece, Italy, Persia, Spain, and France (Gaul). It is said that the Jewish settlement at Alexandria, Egypt, numbered hundreds of thousands. But the real Diaspora (a Greek word meaning "dispersion") came as a consequence of the wars against Rome. While hundreds of thousands of Jews fled the bloodshed and destruction, many hundreds of thousands more were deported as slaves, to every corner of the Roman Empire. There were even Jewish settlements in the Crimea and among the German barbarians.

Partly because Jews did not make good slaves (freedom and independence were tenets of the Jewish religion), and partly because it was the self-imposed duty of free Jews to buy the liberation of those who had fallen into slavery, most Jews in the Roman world were free by the third century A.D. More than that, following the edict of the Emperor Caracalla in A.D. 212, they could become Roman citizens and enjoy almost all the privileges inherent in that title. Furthermore, after the time of Hadrian, they were protected in the practice of their religion. The only disability they suffered was that they, unlike any of the many other races, nations or religions of the empire, had to pay a special annual tax, called the *fiscus judaicus*, which took the place of their annual payments in support of the now-destroyed Temple at Jerusalem. Judaism even acquired a certain popularity among better-educated Romans, many of whom became converts.

But the religion which was destined to conquer the empire was not Judaism, but rather one of its offshoots, Christianity (from the Greek *Christos,* meaning "annointed one" or "messiah"). Based on the teachings of Jesus of Nazareth, a Jewish carpenter executed by the Romans during the upheavals that led to the destruction of Jerusalem in A.D. 66, Christianity was at first indistinguishable from Judaism — especially the Judaism of the Essenes and the Pharisees. In the years following the death of Jesus it was only one of thousands of obscure oriental cults practiced within the empire. The turning point came when a Jewish tent-maker named Saul of Tarsus (later known as Paul) suddenly became convinced of the "truth" of Christian teachings as he journeyed from Jerusalem to Damascus.

Previously he had persecuted Christians — now, with burning faith, great courage, and tremendous ability he became an incomparable propagandist for the new faith. It was due to his efforts more than to those of any other that Christianity assumed the form in which we now know it and ultimately swept the western world. Few Jews in all history have influenced the world to the same extent.

Paul undertook a series of missionary journeys throughout the Roman world to win disciples for his religion. Naturally, he first addressed his efforts to fellow Jews, preaching in the synagogues of the Diaspora. But he gradually became convinced that Christianity would never make real headway among the non-Jewish peoples until it was divorced from Jewish ritual and Jewish law. With great difficulty, Paul achieved an almost complete break with the past. He did away with the ceremonial and ritual regulations of the Old Testament and merged the teachings of Jesus with Greek philosophy and with various mystical ideas currently fashionable in Rome to create a new religion.

Paul's version of Christianity had instant appeal. It was a religion of hope and liberation, denouncing the tyrants of this world and promising redemption in the world to come. It demanded little more than faith and goodness from its followers; it was a Judaism of love rather than stern justice and strict nationalism. To the millions of slaves and oppressed peoples of the Roman Empire it offered comfort.

Despite occasional persecutions, Christianity spread rapidly; by A.D. 313, when the Emperor Constantine the Great issued his famous Edict of Toleration at Milan, it was in ascendancy throughout the Mediterranean world.

But as Christianity grew more powerful it also grew less tolerant — it was not yet sure enough of itself to coexist with rival faiths. And of all the rival faiths in the empire, the

Church Fathers considered Judaism the most dangerous. Not only did Jews and Christians share many basic beliefs; even the ritualistic differences between them were still a little indistinct. So the Church engaged in a continuous effort to create such differences. A whole series of edicts issued by various councils of Christian bishops (especially the one held at Nicaea in A.D. 325) changed various Christian practices (such as transferring the Sabbath from Saturday to Sunday) to distinguish them from those of the Jews. And when, during the fourth century, Christianity became the official religion of Rome, the anti-Jewish attitudes of the Church were elevated into law. In 319 Jews were threatened with burning if they tried to convert Christians; in 339 they were forbidden also to try to convert pagans. Shortly thereafter, marriages between Christians and Jews were forbidden under penalty of death. Finally, under the Emperor Theodosius II (408–450), Jews lost their rights of Roman citizenship. The Code of Theodosius became the basis of later medieval European laws — and it incorporated all the prevailing Christian anti-Jewish misconceptions and prejudices.

Having made Jews noncitizens, Theodosius also permitted their massacre throughout the Mediterranean world. Urged on by fanatical Christian bishops, bloodthirsty mobs eager for plunder burned Jewish synagogues and raged through Jewish communities from Alexandria to Barcelona, from Athens to Rome, murdering untold thousands of Jews and establishing a pattern of Christian behavior toward Judaism which, in various parts of the world, has persisted to our own times.

And when, during the fifth century, the Roman Empire staggered to its death beneath a welter of barbarian invasions, Jews suffered even more. For not only did they partake in the universal misery of a collapsing civilization, but as soon as the barbarians were converted to Christianity, anti-Jewish persecution grew worse than ever. It mattered little whether Jews lived under the Orthodox Patriarchs of eastern Christianity or under the authority of the Catholic popes in the West — their fate was civil degradation, forcible conversion, exile, or death. True, Pope Gregory the Great (590–604) tried to discourage active persecution of Jews. He argued that Jews might be punished for the death of Jesus Christ (by civil degradation and prohibition from marrying, holding public office, practicing medicine, or converting people to their faith), yet since the existence of Jews was standing proof of the truth of Holy Scripture, they should be allowed to practice their religion and to maintain their synagogues. Unfortunately, Gregory's arguments were lost upon the illiterate mobs and the savagely fanatical local bishops who continued to massacre, burn, and pillage Jewish communities. Despite papal edicts, the Jews were expelled from Gaul in 625 and from Burgundy and northern Italy slightly later. The very practice of Judaism was prohibited in Spain beginning in 616. Only in those eastern lands beyond the authority of Christian prelates — in Mesopotamia, Arabia, and Persia — could Judaism continue to flourish, and its days of toleration even there were numbered.

In the spring of the year 622, a moody Arab camel driver named Mohammed, having stirred up the populace with "heresies" and "subversive" doctrines, fled in fear for his life from his native city of Mecca — and the history of Islam began. Mohammed was well acquainted with many of the powerful Jewish tribes of Arabia and well versed in Judaism. In fact, the new religion he preached based itself, like Christianity, upon the Testaments; if anything, the faith of Mohammed was even closer to the tenets of Judaism than was the faith of Jesus Christ. It even copied such essential Jewish rites as circumcision and dietary laws. It recognized the divine inspiration of all the Jewish prophets, especially Moses, and accorded the title of prophet to Jesus. But all the prophets who had gone before were of no significance compared to Mohammed, who was The Prophet and claimed that he, not Jesus was the messiah. Unlike the gentle Nazarene, however, Mohammed taught that those who would not convert to his new faith deserved to be put to the sword.

Like the earliest Christians Mohammed assumed that his words would be well received by Jews — after all, his teachings included much Jewish history and doctrine. But the Jews were no more willing to receive Mohammed as their self-announced Messiah than they had been to accept Jesus in that role. Accordingly, beginning about 624, Mohammed and his followers began to attack the Jewish communities of such cities as Medina and the nomadic Jewish tribes of Arabia. The Jews were systematically expelled, exterminated, or forced to embrace Islam. And the caliphs who inherited the power of The Prophet (following his death in 632) also inherited his intolerance — Jews and Christians were enemies deserving only death.

Under the Caliph Omar, the Arabian tribes burst forth from their peninsula to begin that amazing career of conquest which was to subdue half the western world. Within a very few years, Egypt, Palestine, Syria, Mesopotamia, and Persia — all centers of traditional Jewish culture — fell to the sword of The Prophet. Omar and his successors realized, however, that they could not treat the vast masses of non-Moslems in their newly conquered empire as they had those of Arabia: that would require depopulating the new dominions. So Moslem official attitudes toward Judaism and Christianity underwent a profound change; it was decided that these infidel religions must be tolerated. Tolerated, but not encouraged — Jews and Christians would be required to wear distinctive clothing, would not be allowed to preach their doctrines to Moslems, would be forbidden to bear arms or ride horseback, could not enlarge their synagogues or churches, could not hold public office, and would have to pay a very heavy annual tax.

In short, all the degradations and restrictions imposed upon Jews by Christians were now imposed upon both sects by Moslems — but the Jews and Christians were permitted to co-exist within the Mohammedan domains. Under the impact of the Islamic conquest, the great Jewish centers of learning in Mesopotamia began slowly but steadily to decline, along with the rule of their exilarchs. By the year 1291 they had become extinct. But long before this occurred, most of the Jews of the Middle East had migrated west.

It took the Arabs less than a century to sweep the Mediterranean world from end to end. In 711 an expedition under Tarik crossed the Straits of Gibraltar ("Gebr-al-Tarik," the "Rock of Tarik") and within four years conquered the entire Iberian peninsula up to the Pyrenees. Once again faced with a vast mass of non-Moslem subjects, the caliphs in Spain, as in the Near East, made religious tolerance a cardinal point in their policy. And in Spain, for the first time, the Moslem conquerors began to make a distinction between their Christian and Jewish subjects. It will be recalled that the Christian Visigothic kings of Spain had expelled the Jews in the year 616; therefore, no Jews were to be found in the Christian armies which opposed the Arab conquest. In Spain it was the Christian who was the armed enemy of Islam, not the Jew. Their knowledge of languages made Jews ideal emissaries to the Christian states and their scholarship made them valuable as translators, physicians, and astrologers — whose arts gained them a natural *entrée* to the royal courts of the caliphs.

So began what has been called the Golden Age of Spanish Jewry and of Jewish-Moslem cooperation and even friendship. It produced over the centuries many notable Jewish figures.

There was Hasdai ibn Shaprut (c. 915–970), who was both court physician and unofficial foreign minister for two caliphs; Samuel ibn Nagrela (993– ca. 1063), a poet, scholar, and spice merchant who rose to become grand vizier (prime minister) of the Moslem kingdom of Granada; Isaac ibn Albalia (1035–1094) who was royal astronomer and confidential advisor to the emir of Seville, and a host of others. Nor was it only individual Jews of great talent who prospered under the Spanish caliphate — Jews entered every walk of life and practiced every occupation, rural and urban. Synagogues flourished and the Academy at Córdoba soon eclipsed in reputation even the ancient seats of Jewish learning in the East. To be sure, there were periods of darkness — usually when some new Moslem sect conquered the peninsula, bringing with it the puritanical fervor of the old-style Islam. But the new conquerors would soon discover that they needed their Jewish subjects if they wished properly to administer their new lands and deal with the Christian kingdoms of the north. A mellowing process would begin which inevitably led to renewed tolerance and prosperity for Jews.

The key to all of this was Jewish scholarship. Without it Jews would have been of little use to the Moslem conquerors; with it they enjoyed protection and prestige. But the tradition of Jewish scholarship existed long before Mohammed raised his banners outside Mecca. The central beliefs of Judaism itself implied scholarship: literacy was demanded of all who would study the Old Testament in order to understand God's revealed word. The rabbis of the Babylonian Exile had founded their synagogues not only as places of worship, but also as places of study. And it was scholarship, of course, which had created the Talmud and remained essential to the preservation of that portable nation-in-being. So while other societies might venerate the priest or the warrior, Jewish communities exalted the scholar. Nor was Jewish scholarship narrowly rooted in the study of Jewish lore; the many exiles, the many diasporas Jews had undergone over the centuries had brought them into contact with the art, science, and culture of many lands. Through their translations from the Greek, the Babylonian, and the Persian into Hebrew, Arabic, and, later, Latin, the classical works of antiquity were preserved and spread throughout the western world. While European Christendom sank into dark ages of illiteracy, superstition, and barbarism, the light of civilization was kept burning by Jews and Moslems — especially in Spain.

But the glory of Moslem Spain was not destined to last. The Christian Visigothic kings of northern Spain had never been completely exterminated; beginning in the eighth century they began a seven-hundred-year war to reconquer their homeland — a war that would mold the Spanish character and nation forever. And to accomplish their task they, like the Moslems, enlisted the support of the Jews. Indeed, at the Battle of Sagrajas in 1086, between Alfonso VI of Castille and the Moslems, large numbers of Jews fought on each side (Alfonso lost). But gradually the Christian kings pressed their Islamic enemy farther and farther south, until in 1146 the Moslems begged for help from their North African kinsmen. These were a fanatical sect known as Almohades, who quickly crossed the Straits of Gibraltar, defeated the Christians, and then took over the Moslem kingdoms of the south. The Almohades had no use for the delicate structure of compromise and tolerance that had built a great civilization in Moslem Spain; in every city they conquered, all Jews and Christians who refused to convert to Islam were put to the sword. The synagogues were burned, and the academies, even the great Academy at Córdoba, were destroyed. By the year 1172 not a single professing Jew could be found in all of Moslem Spain; only (ironically) in the Christian north could they find a haven.

Meanwhile, the Jews of Europe north of the Pyrenees, long used to Christian persecution, had gained a respite from their afflictions. For the first time since the barbarian invasions, peace and order had been restored to western Europe — through the conquests and organizing genius of Charlemagne who had himself crowned Holy Roman Emperor in Rome in 800. Charlemagne was both a strong and far-seeing ruler; no one, not even Catholic bishops, dared to disturb the peace of his realm by inciting anti-Jewish riots. Furthermore, the emperor realized that the Jews could be very valuable subjects — for the same reasons the Moslems of Spain found them to be. Accordingly, Charlemagne not only protected the Jews within his vast domains, but also patronized them and encouraged their immigration.

Under Charlemagne and his successors (the Carolingian dynasty and, later, the house of Capet) Jewish communities spread throughout France, into what is now Belgium and Holland, and into Germany — especially the cities and towns of the Rhineland. The Catholic Church did not look with favor upon all this — and indeed spent much time and effort trying to get local civil authorities to enforce the various ecclesiastical codes of restriction against Jews which were adopted with monotonous regularity by various Church councils. But while the Jews enjoyed the protection of the king, these codes were generally neglected. Jewish settlement followed the great trade routes of western Europe — the river valleys of the Meuse, the Rhine, and the Danube — since the Jews carried on most of the trade of the continent. Forbidden by the Church to own land or to hold public office, the Jews found trade as the only outlet for their energies.

The last of the great countries of Europe to receive a Jewish
settlement was England. Although Jewish merchants and traders may have lived there in Roman and Saxon times, the first
real immigration followed upon the heels of the Norman
Conquest of England in 1066. Jews had lived in Normandy
since at least the middle of the tenth century — and it was
natural that some of them accompanied the great duke on his
conquest and that others followed. Soon there were Jewish
communities in London, York, Winchester, and other English
towns.

Jewish settlement in England marked the end of a very
remarkable migration. It coincided with the final decline of
the ancient Jewish communities in the East — in Persia, Mesopotamia, and the Byzantine Empire. To be sure, considerable
numbers of Jews would continue to live in those regions, but
their importance to Jewish history would no longer be central.
From now on, Europe was to be the spiritual as well as the
actual home of Jewish thought, culture, and influence. What
was remarkable about the movement of this people from the
Near East to Europe was not the migration itself (the years
from A.D. 400 to 900 were an age of migration for many peoples) but the fact that of all migrating peoples, only the Jews
were able to carry with them their entire civilization, transferring it from country to country, reinterpreting it in many
different languages, developing it in a host of different envi-
ronments, and seeing it flourish almost instantly wherever it
put down new roots. This achievement was, and has remained,
unique in world history.

The relative security and prosperity of the Jews of western
Europe after the time of Charlemagne ended with the eleventh century. On November 26, 1095, Pope Urban II
preached a mighty sermon to the Church council meeting at
Clermont, France. His Holiness took note that pilgrims re-

turning from the Near East were reporting widespread Moslem desecration of Christian shrines in the Holy Land, and brutal maltreatment of those who tried to visit them. Accordingly, the Pope called upon all of Christendom to rescue Palestine from the hands of the infidels. It has been said that this may have been the most influential speech ever made. It inaugurated two centuries of Christian-Moslem warfare, known as the Crusades, changed the map of Europe and the Near East, opened new trade routes, and, ultimately, new worlds to the European consciousness — and led to centuries of unparalleled suffering for the Jews.

Once long-simmering religious passions were aroused in the illiterate peasants and the bloodthirsty warrior caste who ruled them, they were not to be restricted to one channel. Crusading leaders — monks, barons, kings, and peasants — found it supremely illogical to make war upon the Moslems and leave other opponents of the Christian faith undisturbed. Besides, everyone knew that by killing a Jew one could win remission for sins in heaven and shorten one's time in purgatory. So as the armies and hordes of Crusaders made their way by various routes through Europe to the southern ports from which they were to embark for Palestine, a frightful wave of massacre accompanied their passage. Before the onslaughts of these immense armed mobs, local authorities (who often tried to protect the Jews) were helpless. The Jews of Metz in Lorraine, of Worms, of Mayence, of Cologne, of Trèves, of Prague — an entire litany of cities and towns of martyrdom — fell victim to the insensate rage and lust of desperate throngs. Their homes and synagogues were pillaged and burned, they were torn to bits by the mobs, they were drowned in nearby rivers, they were rounded up and burned alive in public squares — and those who escaped the immediate savagery of the Crusaders were bereft of families, friends, and homes.

The First Crusade passed like a wave of fire through western European Jewry — and when the Crusaders reached the Holy Land and fought their way into Jerusalem, the hills of that city ran with Jewish blood as men, women, and children were put to the sword.

The second Crusade, beginning in 1146, brought a new wave of anti-Jewish violence in its train which brought death to the Jews in several Rhineland cities. That the pillaging and murder were not more widespread was due to the efforts of a saintly monk, Bernard of Clairvaux, whose oratory had inspired the Crusade but who insisted that the Jews not be molested. With the Third Crusade in 1189, the wave of massacre reached England. There, while Richard the Lionhearted was being crowned king at Westminster on September 3, 1189, a mob pillaged and burned the homes of London Jews, murdering many hundreds of them. A little while later the Jews of Norwich, Bury, Lynn, Stamford, and other English towns added their names to the bloody scroll of martyrdom. At York the Jews held out for some time against a mob by taking refuge in the local castle. When at last they saw that they could expect no deliverance they emulated the defenders of Masada. Led by their rabbi, they committed mass suicide.

The taste for blood, now whetted, was not easily appeased. Soon it was no longer necessary to use the pretext of a Crusade to justify the persecution of Jews. All sorts of accusations, one more ridiculous than the other, were now leveled against them. It was whispered that they murdered young Christian children in order to use their blood in sacrilegious rituals; that they ate Christians; that they tortured Christ anew by sticking pins and knives into the Holy Communion wafers that represented His body. It went without saying that they set the fires which regularly consumed medieval towns and caused the pestilences and plagues which recurringly swept the countryside. No matter how idiotic the charge, nor how often princes, kings, popes, or scholars denounced the accusations, the Jews continued to suffer for them. At Blois in 1171, at Paris in 1180, at Erfurt in 1199, at Fulda and Wolfsheim in 1235, at Berlin in 1243, at Paris in 1290, at Brussels in 1370 — the list was endless and would continue to grow through the next two centuries.

Jews were tortured and murdered by the hundreds and thousands in a variety of cruel ways. Of course, they could avoid persecution by accepting the Catholic faith; they had only to be baptized to be immune to the violence which threatened them. Many were — but most were not. Like the Jews of Blois in 1171, most preferred to die in the flames with the sublime confession of their faith on their lips: "Hear, O Israel, the Lord our God, the Lord is one."

While the Jews of France, Germany, and England endured the centuries of tribulation, the Jews of southern Europe, especially Italy and Spain, remained relatively secure. The popes faithfully adhered to the views of Gregory the Great — Jews must be segregated and degraded, but not physically assaulted or forcibly converted. Time after time through these bloody centuries, popes decried the various libels directed against the Jews and denounced their physical persecution. A decree intended to protect Jews against violence, issued by Pope Calixtus II in 1120, was reaffirmed at least twenty-two times by his successors on the Throne of Saint Peter. And in the papal domains around Rome, Jews were safe from the worst extremes of massacre and expulsion. They were also relatively secure in southern Italy, where papal influence was strong — the town of Apulia, near Naples, even became a famous seat of Jewish learning.

But in southern Europe it was still Spain which offered the most prosperous haven for European Jews — no longer Mos-

lem Spain, but now, surprisingly, the Christian Spanish kingdoms. For during the many centuries of the Christian
reconquest, earlier religious intolerance had waned. Christian
monarchs in northern Spain (who often allied themselves with
Moslem principalities in wars among themselves) soon appre-
ciated the advantages to be gained by tolerating a Jewish
population — the same advantages that earlier Moslem rulers
had enjoyed. There were Jewish physicians, translators, diplomats, and scholars employed by the kings of the Spanish
Christian states — and Jews formed important parts of their
armies. By the time of the Almohade conquest of Moslem
Spain in 1146 and their subsequent expulsion of the Jews, very
strong Jewish communities flourished in the north, where
most of the exiles were received.

Most, but not all. Some made their way to the East — and
among them was the greatest Jewish scholar-philosopher of the
Middle Ages, Moses ben Maimon (or, to use the Greek form
by which he was known to the Christian world, Moses
Maimonides). Born in Córdoba in 1135, Maimonides was only
thirteen years old when his native city was captured by the
Almohadan fanatics and its Jewish community scattered. With
his family he wandered through Morocco and North Africa
until finally they settled at Cairo in Egypt. There Maimonides
soon rose to become personal physician to the great Arab conqueror, Saladin. His fame as a scholar spread far and wide, and
from all parts of the Jewish world he was appealed to for
advice. In answer he composed, in Arabic, a masterly commentary on the Mishnah. But the work upon which his fame
was ultimately to rest was his *Guide of the Perplexed,* in which
he reformulated Jewish philosophy, giving it a more rational
basis, reconciling it to the "modern" thought of his time and
placing certain biblical "crudities" in their proper historical
perspective. This great work touched off tremendous con-

troversy among the more orthodox Jews and was soon denounced by the Catholic Church. It nevertheless became a standard handbook for Christian as well as Jewish scholars for centuries to come.

While the Jews of Christian Spain flourished, and their brethren north of the Pyrenees endured martyrdom, very important social and economic changes were occurring which were to fix the mold of Jewish life in Europe until very recent times. They were also to create in Christian minds an image of the Jew which, unfortunately, persists to our own day.

The centuries from the creation of Charlemagne's empire before 800 to the launching of the First Crusade in 1096 saw the emergence and final triumph in Europe of that rigid political, social, and economic system known to us as feudalism. Under its iron-bound hierarchy of serfs, villeins, knights, nobles, bishops, and kings — all owing duties and allegiances to each other in a tangled web held together by Christian oath — there was no room at all for nonbelievers. Jews refused to be land-bound serfs, could not own land of their own, and were, of course, excluded entirely from any rank of the nobility. They could live only in the largest towns and in the cities; they had literally no place in rural areas, whether villages or countryside. But the largest towns and cities were almost always the domain of the king himself. So most Jews came to be known as "king's serfs" in the sense that they owed duty and allegiance directly to the monarch, rather than to any intermediate rank of the nobility. They likewise enjoyed, for what it was worth, the king's protection.

Exclusion from the countryside meant that Jews could earn their livelihood only in city occupations. They were artisans, blacksmiths, bakers, jewelers, carpenters, masons — practicing any one of hundreds of urban crafts — and, of course, they were traders and merchants. But as the feudal order brought increasing security and prosperity to the cities, there began to emerge (around the twelfth century) the system of craft guilds — primitive trade unions and mutual-aid societies. These were, like the feudal society itself, rigidly hierarchical, very exclusive, closed corporations based on specifically Christian doctrines and even generally named after some Christian saint. Jews were, of course, forbidden membership in the guilds — and as the guilds grew more powerful, they became less and less disposed to tolerate competition in their particular craft from Jewish artisans. Over the decades the guilds were granted charters which forbade anyone who was not a guild member to practice the craft of the guild. Thus Jews were systematically cut off from more and more occupations, and their most important activity remained trade, traditionally almost a Jewish monopoly since the downfall of the Roman Empire. The domination of Jewish merchants drew to a close, however, with the coming of the Crusades. Having learned (largely from Jewish sources) the languages and skills of the international merchant, Christians began to develop their own trade routes to the Moslem world. With the Crusades and with Christian dominance in the Mediterranean, the great trading republics such as Venice grew in prosperity. It was not long before Jews were officially excluded from the lucrative Near Eastern trade — and this was followed, during the fourteenth and fifteenth centuries, by the establishment of trade guilds which, enjoying royal protection, drove Jewish merchants out of business.

How could Jews survive? There was one field and one field only left open to them: finance and moneylending. As European trade expanded toward the close of the Middle Ages, a money economy began to replace the older feudal barter system. Craftsmen, merchants, and nobles required money to finance their commercial ventures; kings required money with which to pay their mercenary armies. But according to Catholic doctrine and hundreds of papal decrees, the lending of money at interest was specifically forbidden to Christians — that was usury and usury was a mortal sin. Yet no one — Christian, Jew, Moslem, or pagan — was about to lend out money without demanding some return on it. The problem was neatly solved by permitting Jews the honor of lending money to Christians at controlled rates of interest. As Europe's first merchants, only the Jews had any surplus, lendable amounts of money, anyhow. And as Jewish merchants were excluded from international trade they turned more and more to the last economic role left open to them: moneylending. That became the staple of Jewish business activity — from the pawnbroker who lent a few shillings against a goodwife's iron pot to the syndicate that lent many thousands of pounds against the income of a kingdom. It was largely Jewish money-lenders who financed the construction of the great cathedrals of Europe, the rebuilding of cities, the development of commerce, and, ironically, the Crusades.

Since the Jews everywhere were royal serfs, they soon came to be looked upon by the monarchs as a kind of sponge through which the money of the kingdom could be soaked up. The sponge could then be squeezed whenever the royal treasury ran dry. Taxes and ever higher taxes, enforced loans on a greater and greater scale, outright confiscations — these were the misfortunes of the Jewish moneylenders. And, of course, as the common people saw their money pass through the hands of the Jews on its way into the royal vaults, what might have become hatred of the greedy monarchs was deflected into hatred for the Jews who were forced to do his bidding. Finally, eager Christian bankers and financiers found various ways to get around papal decrees against moneylending and the Church itself somewhat relaxed its bans. By the fourteenth century most high finance was firmly in Christian (mainly Italian) hands, where it has remained ever since. Jews found themselves restricted to small-scale pawnbroking, which, while it earned them only a miserable subsistence, maintained a hateful image among the great majority of poor Christians.

And as the usefulness of Jews as moneylenders to the crown waned and popular religious prejudice against them was fanned to ever greater fury by successive Church decrees, the very presence of the Jew became superfluous to the kings of western Europe, and the final act of the tragedy began to unfold. England, the last of the nations of the west to accept Jews, was the first to expel them. By decree of Edward I in the year 1290, all those Jews who refused conversion were expelled from the kingdom. Some sixteen thousand were thus forced into exile. Shortly thereafter, in 1306, King Philip the Fair of France expelled the Jews from his domains — and one hundred thousand souls joined the ranks of the exiled. In both cases the Jews were almost totally despoiled before they were driven out. They had to sell their houses for whatever they could get (very little under the circumstances); they were, in many cases, forbidden to collect debts owed to them by Christians; they were forbidden to carry gold or silver with them — and they had to pay exorbitantly high taxes to the crown. In short, they were not only exiled, but reduced to abject poverty in the process.

In Germany, political conditions made a total expulsion impossible — there was no German nation, only a collection of many petty principalities. Jews expelled from one of these small states could generally find refuge in another. But if the Jews of Germany were not at this time expelled by universal decree, they were driven to flight by the wave of terror which now broke upon their heads. At Vienna in 1181, Speyer in 1195, Halle in 1205, Erfurt in 1221, Frankfurt in 1241, Würzburg and Nuremberg in 1298, and more than a hundred and fifty other towns, Jews were murdered by mobs or burned alive by civil authorities in scenes of massacre which, in the history of any other country, would have been memorable.

It was in the year 1349 that the anti-Jewish fury reached its height. The Black Death (bubonic plague) was sweeping Europe — killing, eventually, more than one third of the population. It was the greatest scourge in recorded history. Since no natural explanation could be found for the disaster, blame was fixed upon the Jews. They were accused of having concocted a deadly potion of spiders, frogs, lizards, human flesh, the hearts of Christians, and consecrated communion wafers with which they had poisoned the wells of Europe. This was the cause of the terrible contagion!

Idiotic as this charge may sound today, it was sufficient to seal the fate of Jewish communities throughout the Rhineland, Switzerland, and Austria. Whole Jewish congregations were burned to death in their synagogues; the larger Jewish populations of such cities as Basel, Strassburg, Worms, and Cologne were exterminated to the last child. Most of the few survivors of the general holocaust made their way east — to the Slavonic borderlands of the German states and to Poland. There, for a while, they found relative security.

Meanwhile, south of the Pyrenees, the story of Spanish Jewry was rapidly drawing to a tragic conclusion. As the Christian kingdoms consolidated their dominance of the peninsula (by 1350, only a few Moslem strongholds, such as Granada, remained), they had less and less need of their Jewish subjects. The coming of the Black Death stirred up popular anti-Jewish passions and in 1391, beginning at Seville, a wave of murderous riots engulfed the Jews of Spain from Barcelona to Valencia. It is said that more than seventy thousand perished. But these massacres were accompanied by a phenomenon which

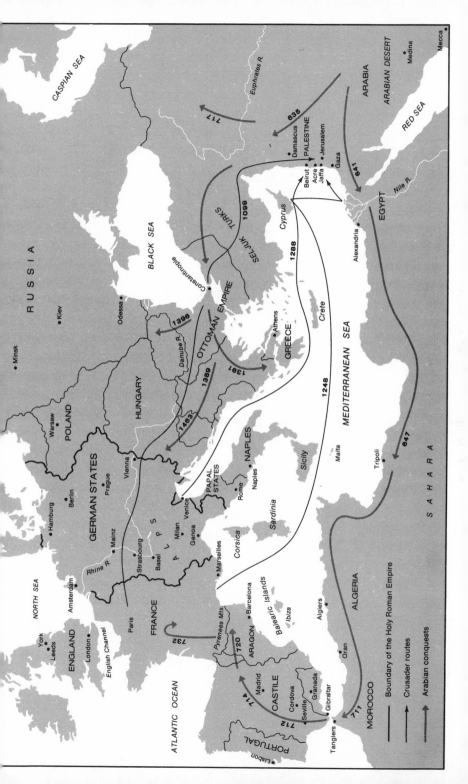

made them unique in western Europe — the wholesale conversion to Christianity of many thousands of Jews.

Throughout all the terrible persecutions to which the Jews of northern Europe had been subjected, very few ever accepted baptism as a way to escape death. In case after case, the Jews remained steadfast to their religion — often committing mass suicide rather than betray it. But in Spain conditions were different. Perhaps because Jewish convictions had been weakened by centuries of well-being, perhaps because Jews had been so well assimilated into Christian life there; perhaps because the recent expulsions in northern Europe left no avenues of escape — for whatever reason, for the only time in Jewish history Jewish morale broke. Many thousands accepted baptism en masse in order to escape death. An entire new class came into being — the *conversos*, those Jews converted to Christianity. But, as will be seen, this apostasy did not long protect them.

When, with the marriage of Ferdinand of Aragon and Isabella of Castille, Spain was united, the new monarchy was faced with the task of ruling a very heterogeneous population: Christians, Moslems, and Jews. During the seven-century crusade of the Christians to reconquer the peninsula from the Moslems, it was religious zeal which united the various Christian kingdoms. In the absence of a national state, only fidelity to the Catholic Church could serve as a test of men's loyalties. Now that a national state had come into being it seemed natural that the allegiance of its subjects be measured by their fanatical devotion to Catholic doctrine. But what of the vast numbers of *conversos* in the realm? These included not only Jews but also Moslems. Were they really sincere in their conversion? Or did they secretly practice their old faiths? With the reluctant permission of the Pope, Queen Isabella set up a kind of Loyalty Review Board to find out. It was called the Spanish

Inquisition and its master was the Queen's personal confessor, Tomás de Torquemada.

Beginning in 1480, the Holy Inquisition embarked on its fearful career of investigating religious conformity. Its first fruits were the burning alive at Seville in a public auto-da-fé (act of faith) of six *conversos*. This was followed by the organization of tribunals throughout Spain — and the smoke of hundreds of ghastly pyres ascended to heaven. No fewer than thirty thousand *conversos* perished in the flames — while many hundreds of thousands more suffered less severe penalties, ranging from confiscation of all their goods to the cutting off of their limbs. Year after year the Inquisition burned its way into the Spanish soul until its very name became a legend of dread. But the irony of this process was not lost upon the Inquisitors themselves — for while they were burning thousands of *conversos,* Jews who remained true to their faith escaped punishment; they were infidels, outside the Church, and therefore could not be guilty of disloyalty to it. This situation was intolerable to Torquemada and his followers and, in 1492, they found a way to remedy it.

It was in 1492 that Granada, the last Moslem stronghold in Spain, fell to the armies of Ferdinand and Isabella. To celebrate and solemnize the victory, the "Catholic Sovereigns" (as they are known to Spanish history) signed an order expelling all Jews from their dominions. Within three months nearly two hundred thousand Spanish Jews fled into exile — leaving behind them not only all their worldly goods but also the memory of a civilization that had been the glory of medieval Europe. Some of the ships carrying Jews into exile set sail on the same tide that was to carry Christopher Columbus over the Ocean Sea to a New World — but the Jews of Spain had no such fortunate landfall.

Where could they go? Northern Europe had already expelled its own Jewish communities; North Africa was a hostile Moslem shore that promised only enslavement. Some of the small Italian states offered refuge — but many of these were under the authority of the Spanish crown. Most Spanish Jews therefore made their way over the frontier into Portugal. But this proved only a temporary haven. In 1497 King Manoel II, "the Fortunate," of Portugal, under pressure from his Spanish neighbors, ordered the expulsion of all Jews from his domains. And with this final blow, the western European stage of Jewish history came to an end for several centuries. Henceforth the center of gravity in Jewish life was to be found in the east — in Poland and, as we shall see, in the Ottoman Empire of the Near East. The Diaspora had come full circle again.

It was during the European Middle Ages that the seeds of that traditional anti-Semitism which still afflicts too many people were first sown. Its growth was due then, as always, to ignorance, misery, and fear. First set apart from his fellow man by the dictates of a Catholic Church which could brook no opposition or competition, the Jew was systematically slandered and pictured as the enemy of mankind by generations of fanatical Christian prelates whose words fell upon the ears of multitudes of totally illiterate, wholly superstitious people, ready to believe anything. Later, with the consolidation of the feudal system, the Jew was legally excluded from any place in society save that of royal serf and moneylender. If the masses of ignorant European Christians did not already sufficiently resent Jewish literacy, Jewish culture, and Jewish knowledge, this forced alliance between Jews and oppressive royal tyrants was enough to arouse universal hatred. For it must always be remembered that bad as was the lot of the Jew during the later Middle Ages, the lot of the Christian was not much better. Life was brutal and short. Most people were serfs — little more than slaves toiling for the benefit of a cruel and rapacious warrior class. If not slain by marauding bands, consumed in endless wars between nobles, driven to starvation by greedy kings, or carried off by endless plagues and pestilences, Europeans of the Middle Ages could look forward only to lives of dull and endless labor. And the Jew, already set apart by Christian doctrine, was a ready-made and defenseless scapegoat for all the misery of the times. He was also a very useful scapegoat for apprehensive kings and bishops — so long as popular passions could be vented on the Jews they might thus be diverted from both the state and the Church. Hatred of the Jews, so fervently preached by Christian churchmen, so cynically manipulated by nobles and kings for so many centuries, finally infected the bloodstream of the European consciousness. It became the mental disease we know today as anti-Semitism.

And what of the dream of Zion during these ages? The greatness of Israel was only a memory now — enshrined in the Talmud and the hearts of Jews. There could be no question of returning to Palestine, long since subject to Islam. So the dream was not one of hope, but rather one of wistful remembrance. It was perhaps best captured in the beautiful lyric poetry of Judah ha-Levi, a Spanish Jew born in 1075, who was a physician and a master of the three cultures of the peninsula — Christian, Moslem, and Jewish. Ha-Levi developed a transcendental passion for the Holy Land and composed heartrending hymns to Zion. Eventually he made his way to Palestine and, after many hardships and adventures, he finally arrived in sight of Jerusalem. In an ecstasy of joy the poet flung himself on the ground and cried out an ode to the greatness of Zion. A passing Arab horseman spurred his steed over the recumbent body, and Judah ha-Levi died still singing the praises of the Holy City.

Haggada:

Saint Valentine's Day, 1349

"In the year 1349 there occurred the greatest epidemic that ever happened. Death went from one end of the earth to the other, on that side and this side of the sea. . . . In some lands everyone died so that no one was left. . . . This epidemic also came to Strasbourg in the summer of the above mentioned year, and it is estimated that about sixteen thousand people died.

"In the matter of this plague the Jews throughout the world were reviled and accused in all lands of having caused it through the poison which they are said to have put in the water and the wells. . . .

"On Saturday — that was St. Valentine's Day — they burnt the Jews [of Strasbourg] on a wooden platform in their cemetery. There were about two thousand people of them. Those who wanted to baptize themselves were spared. Many small children were taken out of the fire and baptized against the will of their fathers and mothers. And everything that was owed to the Jews was cancelled, and the Jews had to surrender all pledges and notes that they had taken for debts. The council, however, took the cash that the Jews possessed and divided it among the workingmen proportionately . . . some gave their share to the Cathedral or to the Church on the advice of their confessors.

"Thus were the Jews burnt at Strasbourg, and in the same year in all the cities of the Rhine, whether Free Cities or Imperial Cities or cities belonging to the lords. In some towns they burnt the Jews after a trial, in others, without a trial. In some cities the Jews themselves set fire to their houses and cremated themselves."

— The Chronicles of the
Rhineland States,
*compiled by Jacob
von Konigshofen.
Translated by Jacob
R. Marcus*

3

The Memory Is Preserved

What! Call ye this Ferdinand "wise" — he who depopulates
his own dominions in order to enrich mine?

SULTAN BAJAZET

An old chronicle tells of how a certain Jew was driven desti-
tute from Spain with his family during the great expulsion of
1492. At sea he lost what little remained to him; his wife was
carried off by pirates and his children were sold into slavery.
"Then," the chronicle relates, "that Jew stood upon his feet,
and spread his hands heavenwards and cried: 'Master of the
Universe! Much hast Thou done to me to make me abandon
my faith. Yet know Thou of a surety that, notwithstanding
Those who dwell on High, a Jew I am and a Jew I will remain!'" The chronicle does not reveal what eventually became of this defiant refugee, but we may assume that he, like
the great majority of his fellow exiles from Spain, Portugal,
and Spanish-ruled southern Italy, sought a haven in the Near
Eastern Moslem world.

That world was changing rapidly. In 1453 the warlike
Ottoman Turks had conquered the remnants of the old Byzantine Empire, including its ancient capital, Constantinople.
The Turks, a military and agricultural people, soon extended
their sway to Syria, Palestine, Egypt, and the Arabian Penin-

58

sula. Although fanatic in their Moslem faith, they did not
bother to persecute the small Jewish communities they found
in their path of conquest. Despising commerce as unworthy of
a warrior nation, they left the trade of their new empire to
subject Jews, Armenians, and Greeks. When the great expulsions began from Spain and Portugal, the Turkish sultans
encouraged the refugees to settle in their dominions. Old
Jewish communities were revitalized and new ones established.
Soon Jewish physicians were ministering to the sultan himself,
Hebrew books (the first books ever to be printed in Constantinople) were appearing, international trade was being
conducted largely by Jews, and Jewish artisans were making a
name for themselves. All the knowledge, skills, and acumen
which had helped to make Spain the most civilized of medieval
societies was now transferred to the Turkish realms. And the
sultans were not slow to employ learned Jews in diplomacy
and as royal counselors.

Take, for example, the case of Joseph Nasi, whose career
reads like a tale from the *Arabian Nights*. His family had fled
Spain to Portugal, Portugal to Antwerp in the Low Countries,
Antwerp to Lyons in France, then to Venice, and finally to
Constantinople. There Joseph Nasi rose to so high a position
in the sultan's court that he became one of the most influential
men in the Turkish Empire — and, since that empire was the
strongest military state in Europe, a force to be reckoned with
throughout the Continent. Nasi recovered the property that
had been confiscated from his family in France by seizing one
third of every cargo sent from France to Egypt; he revenged
himself upon Spain by encouraging the revolt of the Spanish
province of the Netherlands. He repaid Venice for the indig-
nities heaped upon him there by helping to bring about war
between the Turkish Empire and the Venetians, in the course
of which Venice lost the island of Cyprus, of which Nasi almost

became king. He never failed to use his power to protect his fellow Jews abroad, patronized Jewish scholarship and on his death in 1579 left a considerable part of his immense fortune to the Jewish poor of Constantinople.

Another famous Turkish-Jewish statesman, whose career mirrored that of Joseph Nasi, was Solomon ibn Yaish (1520–1603). Of Spanish descent, Ibn Yaish was instrumental in creating the Anglo-Turkish alliance which opposed the ambitions of Spain's Philip II. In close touch with England's Queen Elizabeth, Ibn Yaish sent agents to warn her of the approach of Philip's Invincible Armada and negotiated several treaties with her. The grateful Turkish sultan created him Duke of Mytilene.

Both Joseph Nasi and Solomon ibn Yaish made a gallant attempt to restore a Jewish center in Palestine. After the devastation and massacres of the Arab conquest, the Crusades, and the thirteenth-century Tartar invasions, only a handful of Jews remained in that unhappy land. Yet throughout the centuries pilgrims from Jewish settlements all over Europe had continued to make their way to the former homeland to pray at the tombs of the Patriarchs. Some of them remained to eke out what living they could amid the desolation. And when the Jews were expelled from Spain it was natural that many of them should turn their steps to the still-promised land. In the years after 1492, important Jewish communities were established in Jerusalem, Tiberias, Hebron, and Safed.

Through his influence with the sultan, Joseph Nasi secured the grant of the city of Tiberias (which had long been in ruins) as well as a tract of land surrounding it. Here he proposed to create the nucleus of a semiautonomous Jewish state. Not only did he rebuild the city and its fortifications; he established a textile industry. Mulberry trees were planted for breeding silkworms; merino sheep were imported from Spain;

invitations were dispatched far and wide for artisans and craftsmen to settle in the new colony. Nasi even sent ships to Venice, Ancona, and other Mediterranean ports to bring Jewish immigrants to Palestine. On Nasi's death, Solomon ibn Yaish continued the program — even settling members of his own family in Tiberias. But the time was not yet ripe. Political, economic, and social difficulties beset the experiment, which came to an end with Ibn Yaish's death. Nonetheless, this brave experiment would one day serve as a model for more decisive action. It was the first practical expression of modern Zionism.

Of all the reborn cities of the new Jewish settlement in Palestine, Safed soon became the most important. By the end of the sixteenth century it contained no fewer than eighteen Talmudic colleges and twenty-one synagogues. The scholars of Safed, besides studying the Talmud, endlessly discussed such mystical problems as the origin of the universe and of man and the nature of the unknown. All this lore was known as the Cabala (the Tradition) and had long been handed down from generation to generation by word of mouth. It was considerably enriched when in the thirteenth century a work of great antiquity came to light in Spain. It was called the Zohar (Book of Splendor) and was a mystical — that is to say, cabalistic — commentary on the first five books of the Bible. For the first few centuries after its discovery, the Zohar had little influence on Judaism. But with the onset of the terrible persecutions which culminated in the expulsion from Spain, Jews increasingly sought relief from the miseries of this world in mystical speculation about the next. In Safed, during the sixteenth century, both the Zohar and cabalistic studies slowly came to displace the study of the Talmud itself.

The fundamental conception of the Zohar was that the Law of God can contain nothing trivial, and that every verse, line, word, or even letter of the Bible has some higher, mystical meaning which can reveal, to the persevering student, the mysteries of life. The scholar who became the foremost master of the Zohar and cabalistic speculation was one Joseph Caro (1488–1575), who earned the title Lion of the Cabala in Safed. He composed a famous abridgment of Maimonides' Laws, which won such popularity throughout the Near East that it became the one and only source from which Jewish life was regulated, stereotyped, and — ultimately — devitalized.

From the close of the sixteenth century, Jewish fortunes under the Turkish sultans began to decline. The Ottoman Empire showed signs of decay; weak and sometimes fanatical rulers replaced the brilliant military leaders and statesmen of a former age. With decay came corruption and with corruption, persecution of the Jews. Though there was never any profound change in government policy, no large-scale disaster, nothing that could even begin to compare with the sufferings experienced by Jews under "enlightened" European Christian rule, the Jewish communities in the Near East did not escape the general decay of the Ottoman Empire. Like their Turkish rulers, the Jews of that area slowly slipped into a kind of devitalized slumber which was to last until the First World War.

But in eastern Europe there had come into existence a sturdy and energetic Jewish community — in Poland, the second haven, where, during the terrible persecutions of the fourteenth and fifteenth centuries, Jewish life found a refuge and a breathing space.

Of course, Jews had been settled among the Slavic peoples for many centuries. There were Jewish communities in the Crimea during the first century A.D. — probably traders and migrants from Greece and Mesopotamia. The influence of Judaism had a profound impact upon the pagan tribes of southern Russia. The most important of these were the

Khazars, a people whose kingdom embraced much of the present-day Ukraine. Beginning about the eighth century, impressed by Jewish learning and culture, the still semicivilized Khazars began to convert to Judaism, and by A.D. 780 formed a completely Jewish kingdom, the fame of which spread even to distant Spain. But the Khazar kingdom was short-lived. It was conquered in the tenth century by the prince of Kiev, and its remnants were utterly stamped out by the invading Tartars during the thirteenth century.

The Tartar, or Mongol, invasions of Russia and eastern Europe (1240–1241) changed the course of history in that region. Entire cities were burned, whole populations put to the sword or sent into Asiatic slavery by the hordes of the Khans. Poland was struck with especial severity and, when the Mongol incursions ended, the entire country lay in ruins. Accordingly, from the middle of the thirteenth century the Polish kings began encouraging the wholesale immigration of merchants and craftsmen from Germany. Principal Polish cities were thus repopulated with German immigrants, among them German Jews who redeveloped Polish trade and helped to finance Polish reconstruction. Wave after wave of German Jews, fleeing the terrible persecutions of the Middle Ages, settled in Poland, Lithuania, and the western areas of Russia.

These German-Jewish refugees brought with them not only German culture, but also the German language as it existed during the Middle Ages. This was Middle High German, which, cut off from its source, developed into a separate tongue. Interspersed with Hebrew and Slavic words, written in Hebrew characters, it was known as Jüdisch-Deutsch (Jewish-German) or Yiddish and became the universal language of eastern European Jewry.

By the year 1650, it is estimated that no less than half a million Jews lived in Poland. They dwelt in relative prosperity, security, and even honor, for, with some exceptions, the kings of Poland protected their Jewish community and, like the Moslem rulers of Spain in an earlier age, valued them for their learning and skills. Of course, royal protection was not always sufficient to restrain ignorant peasants or fanatical Catholic bishops; appalling massacres took place from time to time, especially after the onset of the Black Death, when the Jews of Posen and Krakow were wiped out. Yet, by comparison with what was happening to Jews in western Europe, Poland seemed a paradise during these centuries.

An outstanding characteristic of Jewish life in Poland was the remarkable degree of self-government permitted the Jews. In 1551, King Sigismund II Augustus issued an edict allowing the Jews of his realm to elect a chief rabbi and judges with jursidiction over all matters concerning Jewish law. This was most useful to the king because it enabled the Jews themselves to apportion and collect the very heavy taxes with which they were burdened. A natural place for Jewish rabbis and judges to gather, hear disputes between different towns, and try civil cases brought before them was the great trade fairs held yearly in various Polish cities. To these fairs (the most famous was held in Lublin) came Jewish merchants, traders, artisans, and scholars from all over the country. While doing business they could also discuss matters of common interest and reach decisions which, backed by the royal authority, were binding on Jews throughout the kingdom. By slow degrees these trade fair meetings, known as *vaads* (councils), became institutionalized. The Council of the Four Lands (the four provinces into which Poland was divided) met twice a year at the trade fairs held in Lublin and Jaroslaw (Yaroslave). Comprising thirty representatives of Jewish communities throughout Poland, it became a kind of Jewish parliament.

In Poland, as always when allowed a breathing space, Jewish

scholarship blossomed. The rabbis Jacob Pollak, Moses Isserles, Solomon Luria, Joshua Falk, Samuel Edels, Joel Strikes
— all achieved fame and international reputations for their
learning and wisdom. *Yeshivot* (schools) proliferated
throughout the country, and the Jewish child who did not
attend one or another of these was a rarity. Furthermore, Polish Jews did not readily accept the idea that the Law could or
ought to be codified in rigid ways; rather it was to be viewed as
a living source for discussions, debates, interpretations — a
framework within which new ideas could be tested and nour-
ished. Reverting to the basic tenets of the Talmud, Polish
Jewry kept scholarship alive and enjoyed a level of literacy
and education that was unique in all the world. So long as
Poland remained independent, Jewish life there, despite occasional setbacks, flourished.

But while Jewish culture in eastern Europe enjoyed a re-
naissance, the lives of those Jews who survived the persecutions
of the twelfth and thirteenth centuries in western Europe became even more narrowly constricted. As early as the year
1179, a Catholic Lateran Council had forbidden Jews and
Christians to dwell together. This edict was, at first, rarely
enforced. In most cities Jews continued to live where they
pleased, and Christians had little compunction in owning
houses in Jewish quarters. Cities with formal Jewish sections
were in the minority. But in 1516, the city of Venice ordered
that all Jews were to be segregated into a special district. This
area, known as the Getto Nuovo (New Foundry), was expanded soon after by the addition of an area known as the
Getto Vecchio (Old Foundry). Other Italian cities, copying
Venice, called a newly established Jewish quarter a *getto* or
ghetto — the term which we still use to describe any segregated
city quarter, no matter who are its unfortunate inhabitants.
The Venetian example spread not only through Italy but also

to France, Germany, and almost all of western Europe. By the end of the sixteenth century segregation was the common condition of Jewish life.

The ghetto was always walled off from the rest of the city, and its entrance was almost always through a low archway provided with massive doors, guarded by Christian gatekeepers. In larger cities there might be two such entrances, but it was expressly forbidden for there to be more than two anywhere. After nightfall it was considered a serious crime for any Jew to be found outside the ghetto walls or any Christian to be found within. The ghetto gates were also locked on all Christian holy days. But it must not be thought that the early inhabitants of the ghetto found all this utterly detestable, for the walls which kept them in also kept their enemies out.

In many places the ghetto might consist of only a single street or a courtyard; but in the larger cities, such as Rome, Venice, Frankfurt, or Prague, a whole labyrinth of streets and alleys made up a town within a town. Local Christian authorities very rarely permitted any expansion in the area of a ghetto, so to accommodate a growing population, the Jews added stories to already rickety buildings. The reasoning behind this was much the same as that which led to Manhattan's skyscrapers — but the results were far different. Buildings collapsed with depressing frequency. Outbreaks of fire were also especially dangerous in the ghetto — for the whole area might burn to the ground before help could be brought from beyond its walls.

Since Jews were prohibited from owning real estate, even in the ghetto, there would have been no check at all upon the rapacity of Christian landlords had not Jewish scholars recalled the old Hebraic law of *hazakah* (proprietary right). This established, under very severe social and religious penalties, the rights of the actual occupant of a building. No Jew looking for a dwelling was allowed to offer the Christian land-lord more rent than the present tenant paid. Thus, despite increasing population pressures against a fixed supply of hous-ing, Christian landlords were unable to raise their rents. A tenant's "rights of occupancy" in a house or apartment became almost equivalent to ownership — and these rights could be sold or passed on upon death. It was a striking example of how Jewish tradition could adapt itself to deal with new circum-stances, and a remarkable anticipation of tenant-rights laws enacted in crowded modern cities.

Since the ghetto walls were not considered in themselves sufficient to prevent the contamination of Christians by con-tact with Jews, the Lateran Council of 1215 ordered that all Jews were henceforth to wear a badge of a distinctive color. This regulation was not consistently enforced until the six-teenth century — and its form differed from place to place. In Italy, especially the Papal States, Jews were required to wear yellow hats; in Germany they had to wear yellow circles sewn onto their outer garments above their hearts. Any Jew who stirred from the ghetto without such a badge could expect the direst consequences if caught — in many cities Jews were re-quired to wear their badges even within the ghetto. Nor was this the only indignity to which they were subjected.

In many cities, the Jews were tolerated in their ghetto only on the basis of a precarious agreement which had to be re-newed annually. In Rome, every year representatives of the ghetto had to pay homage to the Pope by presenting him with a Scroll of the Law, which the Pope would then return con-temptuously with a derogatory remark. Furthermore, the inhabitants of the ghetto were heavily taxed to support Chris-tian efforts to convert them. Such conversions generally took the form of kidnapping Jewish children for baptism or drag-ging pregnant mothers from the ghetto so that their offspring might be born and baptized in uncontaminated surroundings.

Throughout Germany Jews had to pay a special toll, like the cattle tax, when they crossed the frontiers of the innumerable petty states or entered a city. When they appeared in law courts they had to take an especially degrading and obnoxious oath before testifying. Books printed in Hebrew were regularly confiscated and burned. In Italy it was against the law to possess a copy of the Talmud. In many areas — but especially in Germany — laws were passed forbidding Jews to marry without a special permit, and permits were heavily restricted as a means of keeping the Jewish population down. Often it was only the eldest son of a Jewish household who could marry and build a family.

Most professions (with the exception of medicine) were closed to Jews. So was almost every other occupation. They were not allowed to sell new commodities of any sort, but were permitted to deal only in secondhand wares — which became a typically Jewish enterprise down to very recent times. And since Jews were not allowed to open shops outside the ghetto walls, they were forced into door-to-door peddling — an occupation they came eventually almost to monopolize. Secondhand merchandise, the jewelry trade, pawnbroking: these were the means of livelihood imposed upon the Jews. These and, of course, medicine. For although it was strictly forbidden for Jewish doctors to practice upon Christian patients, the rich, the aristocracy, kings, and popes preferred to turn to Jewish physicians when sickness struck.

Of course the center of Jewish life in the ghetto was, always and everywhere, the synagogue. By law only one synagogue was permitted to any ghetto — and they had to be plain, unadorned buildings of humble dimensions. This by no means meant that some synagogues were not lavishly decorated inside. The synagogues were known everywhere by the name of "school," which was certainly their primary social function. So imbued with the tradition of scholarship were the Jews of western Europe that for centuries Jewish communities as a whole were known to outsiders as "schools." Thus one would refer to the "school of Jews" at Frankfurt much as we refer to a "school" of porpoises.

Perhaps the greatest example of the Jewish scholar produced during the Age of the Ghetto was, ironically, Baruch Spinoza — ironically, because Spinoza, while in his early twenties, renounced the Jewish faith. Born in Amsterdam in 1623, of a family of Portugese Jewish refugees, he soon attained fame as an apt and original scholar. So apt and original, indeed, that the Talmudic studies of the synagogue could not satisfy his wide-ranging and skeptical mind. But then, neither could the narrow scholasticism of Catholic theology. In his greatest work, the *Ethics*, Spinoza developed an almost agnostic view of the universe. That is, he found himself unable either to confirm or deny the existence of God on any rational grounds. Despite the cleverness with which he disguised his conclusions, the *Ethics* was equally repugnant to Orthodox Jews and pious Christians (he never adopted the Christian faith after leaving Judaism). But cosmopolitan Amsterdam was tolerant, even of heretics. Spinoza was left in peace to develop a mind far in advance of its age — one which would have a profound effect upon all subsequent philosophy.

The price paid by European Jews for more than two centuries of ghetto life was severe. Cut off from healthy activity and condemned to permanent poverty, the Jews of Europe lost inches off their physical stature and many years off their life expectancy. Worse than that was the psychological damage. Degrading occupations imposed by law, such as pawnbroking and dealing in old clothes, eroded the Jews' self-respect, while a millennium of the fiercest persecutions made them, predictably, timorous. The restrictions of ghetto life meant that intellectual as well as physical contact with the outside world was at a minimum. Persons of the highest intellectual abilities were forced to pass the whole of their lives in self-contained communities seldom numbering more than a couple of thousand souls. The circle of human interests was suffocatingly confined. How many Spinozas languished in obscurity through these centuries?

In natural response to all this, the Jewish sense of solidarity with fellow Jews became fantastically exaggerated, just as feelings of grievance against the Christian world became almost permanent. Ghetto Jews, over the centuries, lost all sense of proportion. Every specifically Jewish item of daily life, every tradition that had to be defended against a hostile world, assumed greater and greater importance until all things Jewish seemed to weigh equally — the most trivial ceremony with the most fundamental ethical teaching. Superstition increased while scholarship declined. The ghetto was doing its work — destroying Jews and Judaism from within as well as without. The terrible effects of ghetto conditions and segregation suffered by Jews in post-medieval Europe can be compared only to the damage wrought by segregation and ghetto conditions upon Blacks in modern American society. Perhaps this is one reason why American Jews have traditionally been in the forefront of the battle for civil liberties and equal rights in our own time and country.

Meanwhile, beginning in the middle of the seventeenth century, Polish Jews underwent their long hour of agony. In 1648, the Cossacks (nomadic warriors) of the Ukraine rose against the oppression of their Polish rulers. And since Jews often acted as stewards of Polish nobles' estates, or managers of their inns and mills, the Cossack hatred was directed more against them than against their masters. Besides, to the Russian Orthodox Cossacks Judaism was even more hateful than Polish Roman Catholicism. Throughout the country massacres took place on a scale and of a ferocity that beggared anything known in Europe since the time of the Black Death. In city after city — in Nemirov, Tulchin, Ostrog, Lublin, and scores of other places — the entire Jewish community was wiped out. When, in 1654, the Tsar of Russia took the Cossacks under his protection and invaded Poland, the terror increased. In a ten-year period no fewer than one hundred thousand Jews were murdered — and many more driven penniless into exile. Polish Jewry never recovered from these blows. The tide of Jewish migration which had for centuries flowed eastward — from northern Europe during the Crusades, from Spain after the great expulsion of 1492 — now was suddenly reversed. For the next three hundred years, eastern European Jewry would furnish a steady stream of refugees to the West.

It was from the agony of the Polish disaster and the despair of the ghetto that Jews turned in superstitious desperation to a new, self-proclaimed Messiah from the East. This was one Sabbatai Zevi (1626–1676), a resident of the city of Smyrna in Asia Minor. A profound student of the Cabala, Sabbatai convinced himself that he was indeed the Messiah who had so long been awaited by Jews, and whose coming had long been foretold. After a visit to Jerusalem with his half-crazed wife, Sarah (a survivor of the Polish massacres), Sabbatai in 1665 publicly proclaimed himself. And, as befitted his pretensions, he divided Palestine into provinces, which he assigned generously to his friends, who would rule as subordinate kings when he came into his own.

Letters were dispatched to every corner of Europe and Asia announcing the glad tidings. Everywhere Jews rejoiced that the Messiah had finally appeared and the hour of their deliverance was at hand. Prayers were offered in every synagogue on behalf of "the Lord's anointed." The frenzy of the masses knew no bounds. And not only of the masses — merchant princes of Amsterdam declared their faith in the Messiah; English Jews bought passage on ships bound for the Holy Land so as to be on hand for the Great Deliverance. Even the skeptical Spinoza saw no rational reason for doubting that the latter days were imminent. The most eminent and scholarly rabbis assured their flocks that all that had been prophesied in the Old Testament would now come to pass. The princes and kings of the world would acknowledge Sabbatai their overlord; all Jews would be reunited in Palestine and the reign of Jehovah would commence.

Unfortunately, the princes of this world were not prepared to recognize the Jewish Pretender — least of all the rulers of the Ottoman Empire, where the Messiah's presence had stirred serious civil disturbances. When Sabbatai, on the first leg of what he supposed would be a triumphal progress through Europe, arrived at Constantinople, he was arrested and thrown into prison. But this setback made no difference in the eyes of his admirers. After all, was it not written that the Messiah must suffer tribulations before his final triumph? The faithful thronged to visit him in his prison and flooded him with costly gifts.

At last the patience of the authorities was exhausted. Sabbatai was summoned to the Ottoman capital, Adrianople, to appear before the sultan himself. His followers were not dismayed — for now the Great Day for which they had been praying was at hand. They argued amongst themselves about the precise method that Sabbatai would use to reveal his holy mission. Brought face-to-face with the sultan, Sabbatai was offered a choice: he could convert on the spot to Islam or be put to death. Without hesitation Sabbatai chose Islam. He proclaimed his belief in Mohammed and left the sultan's palace a free man with a new name — Mehemet Effendi, a royal pensioner!

This cowardly apostasy did not shake the more devoted of Sabbatai's followers. After all, they argued, the Messiah was supposed to experience every side of human life, even the most un-Jewish, before he could accomplish his mission. Throughout the Jewish world, bands of adherents continued to believe in him. His cult even survived his death in 1676 and until very recent years, believers could be found in Constantinople and other Near Eastern cities. It is possible that had Sabbatai chosen death rather than apostasy he, like Jesus, might have founded a world-conquering religion.

But he did not so choose, and the humiliation of the Jews of western Europe was complete. They were now utterly disillusioned. Never again would they look to a Messiah for redemption. Increasingly they realized that their hopes for salvation depended upon their own initiatives in this world, not the next. The career of Sabbatai Zevi was indeed a sign — not of Jehovah's deliverance, but rather that the age of faith in Jewish as well as Christian Europe was near its end.

Haggada:

How to Teach Children

"If a man has a book in his hand he must not display his anger by pounding on it or by striking others with it. The teacher who is angry with his student must not hit him with it, nor should the student ward off blows with a book unless the blows are very dangerous.

"There once was a student who stuttered and it took him quite a while before he managed to get a word out of his mouth, and when the others laughed at him he would become angry. His teacher, therefore, said to him: 'Don't ask questions in their presence. Wait until they leave, or write down your difficulties on paper, and I'll answer you.'

"It is written in the Bible: 'If thou return to the Almighty, thou shalt be built up, if thou *put away unrighteousness far from thy tents*.' If this is true, why then is it necessary to repeat: 'If iniquity be in thy hand put it far away, and *let not unrighteousness dwell in thy tents*.' It is merely that the Bible wishes to teach us that the teacher shall not say: 'I'll let this mean student remain in order that I may make a better person of him, for he can learn from my good example.' It will be of

74

no avail! It is more probable that he will teach the other children in the house to do wrong.

"When a person teaches children — some of whom are more brilliant than the others — and sees that it is disadvantageous for all of them to study together inasmuch as the brilliant children need a teacher for themselves alone, he should not keep quiet. He ought to say to the parents, even if he loses by making the division: 'These children need a separate teacher; and these, a separate teacher.'

" 'Train up a child in the way he should go.' If you see a child making progress in Bible, but not in Talmud, do not push him by teaching him Talmud, and if he understands Talmud, do not push him by teaching him Bible. Train him in the things which he knows."

— from Judah He Hasid's Book of the Pious, *published in Regensburg in A.D. 1200. Translation by Jacob R. Marcus*

4

The State Is Denied

> The vineyards of Israel have ceased to exist but the eternal Law enjoins the children of Israel still to celebrate the vintage. A race that persists in celebrating their vintage, although they have no fruits to gather, will regain their vineyards.
>
> BENJAMIN DISRAELI

By the middle of the eighteenth century the ghetto walls of Europe were beginning to crumble. They were being undermined by the economic necessities of a new age struggling to be born: the age of mercantile capitalism, of industrialization, of colonial expansion, of skepticism and the scientific method. They were being ridiculed out of existence by the angry laughter of a new breed of rationalists such as Voltaire, Rousseau, and the *philosophes* of an approaching revolution. They were being battered by new winds of thought in Christian Europe — for the ghetto walls of men's minds had first to fall before the stone ramparts themselves. The ghetto mentality — of those within as well as those outside its gates — was one of many feudal chains shrugged off in the birth struggles of the Age of Reason.

It had all started centuries before, in 1492. "And thus," wrote Christopher Columbus (himself probably of Jewish extraction), "having expelled all the Jews from all your kingdoms and dominions, in the same month . . . Your Highnesses commanded me that, with a sufficient fleet, I should go to the said parts of India. . . ." At the very moment when a new era of persecutions opened for the Jews, the seeds of that intellectual revolution which would one day enlighten their persecutors were planted. And just as Columbus, at a stroke, expanded the physical world in European consciousness beyond men's wildest imaginings, so the work of Galileo, Newton, Descartes, and a host of post-Renaissance thinkers shattered the closed world of Catholic dogma and popular superstition.

The Protestant Reformation of the sixteenth century also modified popular attitudes toward Jews — generally for the better. The various Protestant churches emphasized the Bible (rather than the Pope) as the source of all revelation and wisdom. The Jews, as the ancient people of God and the "People of the Book," were regarded with greater favor by Protestant divines than by Catholic bishops.

And as always, the skills, learning, and aptitudes of Jews remained of the highest value to European rulers throughout the ghetto era. Thus, while all Jews had been expelled from England and France during the thirteenth century, some few were permitted almost immediately to return — as physicians to the royal families, as financial advisors, sometimes as highly skilled artisans. In England, typically, the status of these Jews was kept cloudy, their existence neither approved nor condemned. In France the settlement of Spanish refugee Jews in the south, as well as the existence of a large community of German Jews in Alsace was officially recognized — but rarely discussed. In Holland (which then included most of present-day Belgium) Jews were not only officially tolerated, but encouraged in their commercial ventures. Jewish merchants dominated the international trade of the great port of Amsterdam. In Germany, after the end of the Protestant-Catholic religious wars of the sixteenth and seventeenth centuries, Jews were increasingly allowed to settle outside the ghettoes. Almost every petty German principality counted Jewish physicians and advisors among those closest to the sovereign. Even in Italy (except in the Papal States, where medieval thinking and law were preserved down to the twentieth century) conditions for Jews were slowly improving. The gates of the ghettoes in cities like Venice and Genoa were no longer closed with any great punctuality — and the wearing of the special Jewish badge was no longer enforced.

The new position of the Jew in European society was typified by the career of Moses Mendelssohn (1729–1786). Born in the ghetto of Dessau, Germany, the young Mendelssohn had sharpened his wits by poring over the Talmudic texts. In 1743 he went to Berlin to study mathematics, Latin, and modern languages. He supported himself by tutoring and bookkeeping and finally became manager for a Jewish manufacturer. In 1763, to the utter astonishment of everybody, he won a prize awarded by the Prussian Academy of Sciences for an essay on metaphysics.

Mendelssohn became famous. To Germans, the phenomenon of a Jew who could write German (as opposed to Yiddish) with sufficient grace to win so prestigious an award was remarkable. Rich and influential Berliners took him to their bosoms, and he was even advanced to the rank of "protected Jew" by the Prussian government.

Emboldened by all this, Mendelssohn, in his writings, tried to reconcile Judaic thought and tradition with the new and liberal ideas which were sweeping the world beyond the ghetto walls. He published a new edition of the Pentateuch with a translation into excellent German and an up-to-date commentary in pure, classical Hebrew. The commentary not only gave a powerful impetus to Hebrew letters (it may be considered the beginning of modern Hebrew poetry, essay, and drama), but also went far beyond the rigid Talmudic teachings which had limited Jewish thought.

Unfortunately, Mendelssohn's influence upon Judaism was not altogether beneficial. The breaking down of barriers between Jews and non-Jews resulted in assimilation — the Jews' abandonment of those aspects of their culture and traditions which distinguished them from their fellow citizens. The logical end of that process was conversion to Christianity. Although Mendelssohn himself remained scrupulously faithful to Jewish practices, his daughter married a Christian and his grandson Felix Mendelssohn, baptized in infancy, used his genius to enrich the music of the Christian church.

Among European ruling classes Mendelssohn's career aroused great interest. The "enlightened despots" of the Age of Voltaire, such as Catherine the Great of Russia, Frederick the Great of Prussia, and Joseph II of Austria, began to believe that with a little encouragement, every Jew might show himself to be a Mendelssohn and in the end — who could tell? — the age-old problem might be solved by wholesale assimilation.

Joseph of Austria (influenced by a former pupil of Mendelssohn's) in 1781 abolished the special Jewish poll tax and the wearing of the Jewish badge. The following year he issued a general decree of tolerance. Although there was no question of placing Jews on an equal footing with Christians before the law, the principle was declared that restrictions upon them should be gradually removed and they should be allowed to mix more with the general population. Ecclesiastical anti-Jewish regulations were abolished and Jews were encouraged to take up various crafts and agriculture and the public schools were declared open to them. (However, in 1788 all Austrian Jews were ordered to adopt a proper, recognizable surname, rather than the Biblical patronymic which had been traditional. If any Jew hesitated, then a name was created for him and registered — often with intentionally ridiculous results.)

Joseph II's example was followed elsewhere. In 1784 Louis XVI of France abolished several important abuses, including the "tax of the cloven hoof," imposed on Jews and cattle at every toll house. In Tuscany the Grand Duke Leopold I included Jews in the scope of his widespread reforms. Of even greater importance, when Austria, Prussia, and Russia conquered and partitioned Poland during the latter half of the eighteenth century, the Prussian and Austrian reforms were automatically extended to the great multitudes of Polish Jews who now came under their rule. Those Polish Jews who found themselves living under Russian sway were not so fortunate, as we shall see.

It was in the midst of these sentimentally inspired and unrealistic, if welcome, "reforms from above" that the bombshell of the French Revolution burst. Inspired by the same liberal impulses that had begun eroding the social fetters of the Jews, the revolutionaries proclaimed Liberty, Equality, and Fraternity among *all* men. The famous Declaration of the Rights of Man, shouted from the tribunals of the Convention, had as its logical corollary the emancipation of the Jews. But logic does not necessarily go hand-in-hand with nobly proclaimed ideals. The American Declaration of Independence (which partly inspired the French revolutionists) had, a decade earlier, proclaimed that "all men are created equal." Yet Black Americans remained enslaved. It required a hard fight against broad opposition before the new French revolutionary government extended the Rights of Man to Jews. But at last, on September 27, 1791, French Jews were fully emancipated. For the first time in the history of modern Europe, Jews were formally declared to be citizens of the country of their birth.

And wherever the French Republican armies penetrated —

into Holland, Italy, Austria, and the German states — they carried the Revolution — and Jewish emancipation — on their bayonets. In Holland Jews were granted full citizenship in 1796 — and a year later Jews were elected members of the National Assembly. In Italy, city after city broke down the ghetto barriers as French forces approached. In Venice on July 10, 1797, the ghetto gates were torn off and burned amid great popular jubilation; in Rome the ghetto walls fell a year later, in February, 1798. Everywhere Jews formed part of the new municipal governments. In Germany events moved unevenly. In the Rhineland, as in Italy, Jews were emancipated on the first appearance of French troops, but in other sections their freedom was delayed. When Napoleon Bonaparte organized the conquered German principalities into the Confederation of the Rhine in 1806, Frankfurt became its capital. But it was not until 1811 that the important Jewish community of that city was granted full emancipation. In Prussia, Jewish freedom was not won until 1812, and then, still, government office remained closed to them.

Unfortunately, like the French Revolution itself, all of this was something of a false dawn. The French middle classes (and, following them, other European bourgeoisies) had roused the long-suffering workers and peasants to destroy feudal aristocracy and break the ancient political fetters which prevented middle-class economic advance. But when these same workers and peasants, in their revolutionary zeal, began questioning the rights of property itself and calling for economic as well as political democracy, the now-dominant French and European bourgeoisies recoiled. This explained Napoleon's rise to power in France — not to consummate, but rather to put an end to, the Revolution before it should undermine the newly won supremacy of the middle class. But the rule of this military adventurer brought in its train a generation of continent-wide warfare, ruinous to trade and industry. So when the emperor was finally defeated and the representatives of the powers met at the Congress of Vienna in 1814, their entire energies were devoted to finding a formula whereby political reaction (the restoration of the monarchies destroyed by the Napoleonic Wars) might be accommodated to the expanding energies of an emerging capitalist system.

And Jews were certainly prominent among the new middle-class capitalists. Take for example, the Rothschilds of Frankfurt. The founder of the family, Meyer Amschel (1743–1812), had built up a lucrative brokerage business in Frankfurt as an agent for the local ruler: the Landgrave of Hesse-Cassel. The family house in the Frankfurt ghetto, like so many others, had for generations been identified by a sign hanging outside — in this case a red shield. It was from the German for "red shield" that the family took its name. Amschel's third son, Nathan Rothschild, went to England in 1796 and entered the cotton business in Manchester. But he soon moved to London, where he achieved power and fame as a banker. Nathan Rothschild negotiated loans for the British treasury, shipped gold to Spain to pay Wellington's armies, and organized an intelligence service so perfect (it used carrier pigeons) that he was able to give the British government itself the first news of the victory over Napoleon at Waterloo. When peace came, Nathan's brothers, with his help, set up as bankers in Paris, Vienna and Naples as well as Frankfurt. Soon the house of Rothschild became, as Metternich observed, the sixth Great Power of Europe. No great enterprise was possible without their support; no important loan could be floated without their cooperation.

Nor were the Rothschilds alone among important Jewish banking families. There was the house of Goldsmid in England, the Péreire family in France, the Bischoffsheims of

Mainz, London, Paris, Amsterdam, and Brussels and others.
Just as the Jews of the Middle Ages had financed the creation
of European nation-states, so Jews of the nineteenth century
financed the emergence of industrial capitalism. But the interests of the relative handful of Jewish financiers who enjoyed
the protection of their wealth and the friendship of their important (often royal) clients were, essentially, those of the
ruling rich. They welcomed stability in European politics —
even when that stability was bought at the price of reaction, as
it was at Vienna.

Thus, when the Congress of Vienna created a new German
Confederation, although lip service was paid to the newly won
emancipation of the Jews, the individual principalities and
free cities of the confederation followed their own sometimes
harshly reactionary policies. The cities of Bremen and Lübeck
expelled all recently settled Jews; Frankfurt signed a fairly
liberal pact with its Jewish community in 1824; Prussia maintained twenty different codes of Jewish status in its various
provinces. In Germany conditions ranged from almost complete freedom to semimedieval segregation.

In Italy the reactionary backlash was severe. Lombardy and
Venice reimposed anti-Jewish regulations. In the Papal States
the ghetto system was reinstated down to the last detail. In
Bavaria in 1819 mobs shouting *"Hep! Hep!"* (the initials of
Hierosolyma est perdita — Jerusalem is lost — a traditionally
anti-Jewish cry since the days of the First Crusade) attacked
Jewish quarters in various cities. Young Jewish intellectuals
like Heinrich Heine, the poet, despairing of ever being able to
make their way in a hostile Christian world, cynically accepted
baptism as the price of emancipation. Only in France and Holland were the legal and constitutional rights of Jews maintained.

Yet no matter how drastic the reaction after the Napoleonic

Wars, there was everywhere a subtle difference between the old regimes and the new. Before the French Revolution, restrictions upon Jewish life had been universal, and opportunities were the exception. Now opportunities were many, though still qualified by restrictions. The Jew was no longer an inferior, degraded being, marked off from his fellow humans by dress, language, and occupation. He had breathed the air of freedom for the first time in more than one thousand years; his horizons had widened. He had attained the status of a man, at least — although it still remained for him to attain the status of a citizen. No matter what repressive legislation was introduced, it was now impossible to set back the clock of progress. It was through a revolution that all this had been accomplished; no wonder then that many Jews threw themselves heart and soul into every revolutionary movement of the nineteenth century.

Jews were in the forefront of the revolutionary wave which swept Europe in 1848. They fought for Polish freedom under Kosciusko, bled for Hungarian independence with Kossuth, and accompanied Mazzini and Garibaldi in their fight for Italian unification and freedom. Everywhere European liberals set as their goals constitutionalism and religious liberty, and where these were established, Jews won full emancipation — in France in 1830, in Austria-Hungary in 1867, in Italy in 1870, and in the new German Empire in 1874. Only in England and America was Jewish freedom established peacefully, rather than as a part of bloody revolutionary struggles.

In England, ever since Jews had begun to resettle under Cromwell's dictatorship, their social and economic emancipation had been almost complete. They were not forced into ghettoes, did not have to wear badges, lived wherever they pleased, mixed freely in Christian society, and could enter all but a few occupations. The political restrictions against Jews were much the same as those against Catholics and dissenting Protestant groups who were not members of the state church: the Church of England.

But liberal sentiment grew in England after the Napoleonic Wars and, beginning in 1833, bills for the complete emancipation of the Jews were passed by the House of Commons almost every year — only to be rejected with depressing regularity by the House of Lords. Meanwhile Jews were admitted to the practice of law in 1833, and were permitted to hold municipal office in 1845. Some were knighted, while Benjamin Disraeli, a baptized Jew proud of his ancestry (to which he never failed to refer) won a foremost place in the councils of the Tory Party. Time and again Baron Lionel de Rothschild was elected to Parliament by the City of London, only to be refused admittance. When Sir David Salomons, elected a Member of Parliament by Greenwich in 1851, attempted to occupy his seat he was expelled and heavily fined. Finally, in 1858, the House of Lords retreated from their last-ditch stand and Jews were permitted to sit in Parliament. In 1871 the few remaining religious restrictions were removed and Jewish emancipation in England was complete. Benjamin Disraeli, now Lord Beaconsfield, became the first English Prime Minister of Jewish descent.

In the New World Jews had enjoyed relative freedom almost from the beginning. Nor was this entirely fortuitous. For not only was Columbus himself most probably of Jewish descent, but his enterprise was financed by several "New Christians" or *conversos*. Luis de Torres, a Jew who had been baptized the very day Columbus sailed, was the first European to set foot in the new land — and, alas, the first to use tobacco. *Conversos* (most of whom secretly continued their Jewish faith and traditions) emigrated in large numbers to Spanish America; they were among the *Conquistadores* who subdued Mexico, Peru, and the rest of South America.

In 1654 a small party of *converso* refugees arrived at New Amsterdam (as New York, then under Dutch rule, was called). Here they were allowed to settle so long as "the poor among them do not become a burden . . . but be supported by their own Nation." Soon this little colony grew and, reinforced from time to time by new immigration from Europe or South America, spread to neighboring regions. By 1750 Jewish communities existed in New York, Newport, Philadelphia, Savannah, Charleston, and elsewhere. Mostly their members engaged in the import-export trade, though not a few were ship-owners. Of Aaron Lopez of Newport (d. 1782), it was said that for "honor and extent of commerce, he was probably surpassed by no merchant of America."

The handful of two thousand Jews then to be found in the Colonies played an important part in the American Revolution. The names of Francis Salvador ("scalped by the Indians"), Major Benjamin Nones, Captain Jacob Franks, and, above all, Haym Salomon, an immigrant Polish Jew who performed miracles of finance to keep Washington's ragged army supplied, attest to the devotion of colonial Jews in the cause of liberty. As in England itself, the Jews of colonial America had been subject to few restrictions. The Constitution of the United States, which declared that no religious test should be required as qualification for any public office, removed even these. Nonetheless, local prejudice kept Jews from exercising their rights in Maryland until 1825, in North Carolina until 1868, and in New Hampshire until 1877.

When peace was restored to Europe after the Napoleonic Wars, the trickle of Jewish immigration to the New World became a stream. Although Jews from every European country

made their way to America, it was German Jews who predom-
inated in the years before the Civil War. Some of these were
refugee radicals fleeing police persecution after the lost Revolution of 1848. But most came to the New World seeking the
same benefits as non-Jewish immigrants: political and social
freedom and economic opportunity. By midcentury there were
small settlements of Jews in every important town and city,
from New York to San Francisco. In New York there were
three German-Jewish synagogues alone. These synagogues
took the lead in establishing, as a common meeting-ground for
all American Jews, the Independent Order of B'nai B'rith
(Sons of the Covenant), which, during the next hundred
years, would become an institution of national importance.

By the time the Civil War rent the fabric of the nation, Jews
were becoming fully incorporated into American life. More
than ten thousand of them fought and died in the terrible
battles of that war. It is, perhaps, an indication of how fully
they were assimilated into their surroundings that, although
Judaism, both religiously and ethically, has always been opposed to slavery, a Jewish lawyer, Judah Benjamin (1811–
1884) served successively as Attorney-General, Secretary of
War, and Secretary of State in the Confederate government. It
was already obvious that the assimilation of American Jews
was going to lead them away from older European traditions
of religious orthodoxy.

But then, the dream of assimilation in Europe, as well as in
the New World, was leading Jews into paradox and inconsis-
tency. Assimilation — that is, the melting of Jews into the
general population and life of Christian nations — was a
shared dream. It was not only the dream of a people who had
been rigorously excluded from the world outside the ghetto; it
was also the dream of "enlightened" Christian governments
and political leaders. It was regarded as the ultimate solution

to the "Jewish Question." But the social and economic framework of the society into which Jews were to be assimilated was
one that created problems for some Jewish consciences.

Christian society, it seemed, was willing to "accept" exceptional Jews in much the same way that medieval kings had
accepted "court Jews." The Péreire family in France enjoyed
the respect of everyone — and why not? They financed the construction of the French and German railway systems. But
when those systems went into bankruptcy it was Péreire the
Jew rather than Péreire the financier who was blamed. And
not only in banking, but in every field, Jewish "tokenism"
became widespread during the nineteenth century. In part
this was due to the unshackling of traditional Jewish scholarship. For centuries, Jewish thought had been sharpened on
religious and ethical studies while at the same time being excluded from contact with the new technology of the industrial
age. When that thought was finally liberated — when Jews
were admitted into secular universities and into the main-
stream of European development — the intellectual pressure
cooker of the ghetto exploded with remarkable results.

The names are too numerous even to summarize: names
like Ehrlich, conqueror of syphilis; Haffkine, the world's
greatest bacteriologist, whose research into bubonic plague
saved millions of lives; Lombroso, founder of modern crimi-
nology; David Ricardo, the great English economist; Maurice
Loewy, the astronomer. The first navigable airship was con-
structed by David Schwartz, the first motorboat by Moritz
Jacobi. Siegfried Marcus helped pioneer the automobile. The
safety match was invented by Sansone Valobra, the micro-
phone by Emile Berliner; the development of color photogra-
phy owed much to Gabriel Lippmann. The Ullstein family in
Germany became the lords of German publishing, while
Baron Paul Julius von Reuter created the world's greatest

news agency. Albert Ballin, founder of the Hamburg-Amerika steamship line, did more than any other individual for the development of Germany's merchant marine, as did Emile Rathenau for the development of Germany's electrical industry. Ludwig Mond established the English alkali industry; his son Alfred developed a major British chemical industry.

There was, it seemed, no field in which the liberated Jew could not establish himself. Sarah Bernhardt and Max Reinhardt revolutionized theater; painters like Israels, Liebermann, Pissaro, Modigliani, and Chagall, sculptors like Epstein, philosophers like Henri Bergson — all left indelible impressions in their fields. Boxing, the creation (in its modern version) of Daniel Mendoza, was long dominated by Jews. Even the humane treatment of animals enlisted Jewish interest — Lewis Gompertz began the movement (in 1824) which eventually led to the creation of the S.P.C.A. And by the end of the nineteenth century Sigmund Freud was completing work on his new theory of psycho-analysis, while a young Albert Einstein was interesting himself in physics. There could be no question that for the exceptional or gifted Jew, all fields were open, all possibilities endless — at least in western Europe and the New World.

But just as the development of the industrial age raised some Jews to the heights of success and prosperity, it assimilated the vast majority into the universal misery of the new industrial working classes. Péreires might build railroads, Ullsteins might create publishing empires, Prime Minister Benjamin Disraeli might buy the Suez Canal for Great Britain with money advanced by the Rothschilds — but the industrial proletariat into which the great majority of newly emancipated Jews were forced remained harshly exploited.

An observer of that exploitation at first hand was Karl Marx, who spent most of his life in England — having fled the failure of the German revolution of 1848. Marx was a descendant of a long line of famous Jewish rabbis in his home town of Trier. The family, like other German Jews, had been emancipated in the flush of French revolutionary conquest. But when, following the Congress of Vienna, reaction again settled upon German Jewish communities, Marx's father, to protect his new-won position, adopted Christianity. But although Marx was baptized at the age of six, he could not escape his heritage. His investigations into the details of industrialization, of prices, wages, profits, and the misery of the poor were reminiscent of the painstaking work of Talmudic scholars debating the meaning of a single word, a comma, a period. And the thunder of his condemnation of capitalism echoes the thunders of those Old Testament prophets who laid down the law to the kings of Judah. An atheist himself, Marx viewed the "Jewish Problem" (as he viewed everything else) as merely one of the inevitable results of the economic and social organization of the feudal world. Jewish emancipation was no more than an episode in the destruction of feudalism by the economic and social forces of the new industrial capitalism which supplanted it. When capitalism itself had been destroyed by the approaching revolution of the exploited working classes, then Jews, like all other workers, would be truly free. In fact, in a socialist or communist society there would be neither Christians nor Jews, since religion itself would be discarded. Marxism or (as its inventor called it) "scientific socialism," promised total assimilation with a vengeance.

But in this respect, at least, Marx was simply reflecting the ideal of his age of Jewry — complete assimilation. Judaism was, after all, only another religion, like Christianity or Taoism or Hinduism — and with the breaking of social and economic barriers through industrialization, and the breaking of ancient prejudices through popular education, it was inevitable that within a very near future all Jews would become indistinguishable from their fellow citizens of different faiths. Modern societies wished it so, history had decreed it, and Jews themselves, after their centuries of segregated life, worked fervently toward this end.

So hard did they work, in fact, that attachment to Judaism itself dwindled (in western Europe and the United States) throughout the nineteenth century. Synagogues which once had been filled to overflowing three times a day were now often empty except for the most important holidays; the strict observance of orthodox rites and rituals in the home began to be relinquished; in many cases, even the Sabbath was no longer observed. Knowledge of Hebrew and of Talmudic lore was reduced to a minimum. It is estimated that no fewer than two hundred thousand Jews went so far as to have themselves baptized during the nineteenth century in western Europe. And those who were not baptized were often at pains to describe themselves as English, French, or German of the "Jewish persuasion," not members of a different group whose history, religion, and ethnic culture made them a people. And in all of this the ancient ideal of a national restoration to Palestine played no part. To assimilationist Jews this was now superfluous, unnecessary, undesirable. Each in their European or American homeland said: "This land is our Palestine, this city our Jerusalem, this synagogue our Temple." And they might have added; "Nineteenth-century romantic liberalism is our Messiah." The dream of Zion had not simply faded — it was now vigorously denied.

Haggada:

The Jews of New York in 1748

"Besides the different sects of Christians, there are many Jews settled in New York, who possess great privileges. They have a synagogue and houses, and great country-seats of their own property, and are allowed to keep shops in town. They have likewise several ships, which they freight and send out with their own goods. In fine, they enjoy all the privileges common to the other inhabitants of this town and province.

"During my residence at New York . . . I was frequently in company with Jews. I was informed, among other things, that these people never boiled any meat for themselves on Saturday, but that they always did it the day before; and that in winter they kept a fire during the whole Saturday. They commonly eat no pork; yet I have been told by several men of credit, that many of them (especially among the young Jews) when travelling, did not make the least difficulty about eating this, or any other meat that was put before them; even though they were in company of Christians.

"I was in their synagogue last evening for the first time, and this day at noon, I visited it again, and each time I was put into a particular seat, which was set apart for strangers or Christians. A young rabbi read the divine service, which was partly in Hebrew, and partly in the rabbinical dialect. Both men and women were dressed entirely in the English fashion; the former had all of them their hats on, and did not once take them off during service. The galleries, I observed, were appropriated to the ladies, while the men sat below. During prayers, the men spread a white cloth over their heads, which perhaps is to represent sackcloth. But I observed that the wealthier sort of people had a much richer sort of cloth than the poorer ones. Many of the men had Hebrew books, in which they sang and read alternately. The Rabbi stood in the middle of the synagogue, and read with his face turned towards the east; he spoke, however, so fast, as to make it almost impossible for anyone to understand what he said."

> — *Peter Kalm, a Swedish*
> *tourist in New York,*
> *1748. Translation by*
> *Jacob R. Marcus*

5

The Dream Is Reborn

The emancipated Jew has no sense of security in his human relations, he is timid with strangers, he is even suspicious of the secret feelings of his friends. . . . He becomes an inner cripple.

MAX NORDAU

The warm sun of liberalism, of Liberty, Equality, and Fraternity, set early for the Jews of Europe. The high noon of their emancipation and "acceptance" by Christian society was, perhaps, 1870, when religious liberty was officially established in the new German Empire, in Austria-Hungary, Switzerland, Sweden, and Rome. That very year the new French Empire of Louis Napoleon extended the principle of religious freedom to their colony of Algeria, thereby carrying the conception for the first time into the Moslem world. The dawn looked bright — but night fell swiftly.

Of course there had always been, in all countries, reactionary elements which opposed Jewish emancipation. But their voices had been stilled by the waves of revolution. And since religious tolerance (meaning, primarily, tolerance between Catholics and Protestants) was now woven into the fabric of European society, it was impossible to whip up anti-Jewish feeling on the old theological grounds. When, after 1870, the voices of hate were again raised, they sang a new tune. While professing to respect Judaism as a religion, they attacked Jews as a "race."

Ernest Renan, the brilliant French historian, first popularized the conception of "Semitic" and "Aryan" as racial terms. The words originally had been used to distinguish two families of languages from each other. Renan himself did not consider the Jews to be Semites, and doubted whether they even constituted a distinct "race." But his writings fell upon fertile ground in Germany, where reactionaries seized upon them as a cover for their old prejudices.

The anti-Semites (as they were named in 1879 by German pamphleteer Wilhelm Marr) insisted not only that Jews belonged to a distinct "race," but that this race was degenerate — which, in view of Jewish eminence in the arts, sciences, politics, and life of the times, was demonstrably stupid. And disregarding the fact that most of the important nations of Europe had come into existence comparatively recently, while the Jews had been there for two thousand years, they denounced Jews as "aliens" in European life. Jews were inferior, it was claimed, to their fellow citizens of Aryan (and more specifically of Teutonic or Nordic) "race." Furthermore, the Jews were responsible for every trouble and all misfortunes. If they succeeded in any field it was only because of their conspiracy to dominate the world. The German historian Heinrich von Treitschke fanned the flames of hatred when he spoke of the Jews as "Germany's misfortune." Certain German theologians even tried to prove that Jesus Christ could not have been a Jew.

The new anti-Semitism gained momentum in Germany after 1873, when the wave of prosperity which had followed German victory in the Franco-Prussian war of 1870 ended in a crash and subsequent depression. Looking for a convenient scapegoat for their miseries, people siezed upon the Jews. A

number of yellow-press pamphleteers like Marr and Eugene
Duhring found they could make a living by grinding out anti-
Semitic propaganda. But no great importance was attached to
their agitation until 1879. In that year, Otto von Bismarck, the
German Chancellor, decided that the tide of democracy had
advanced too far in the new German Empire. In his efforts to
stem it he allied himself with the reactionaries. The Jews, in-
debted to liberalism and democracy for their emancipation,
had always been foremost in the fight against reaction, and
thus were one of the prime targets of Bismarck's struggle to
stamp out liberalism.

Under Bismarck's protection the anti-Semites began demanding restrictions on the Jews, and the anti-Semitic movement which would one day culminate in the greatest tragedy
in human history was born. Books reviling the Jews poured
from German presses; deputies to the German Reichstag made
anti-Jewish speeches; a newly organized anti-Semitic League
presented a petition to Bismarck demanding that Jews be rele-
gated to second-class citizenship. The petition bore the signa-
tures of 255,000 people. Anti-Jewish riots took place in various
cities after 1881, including the capital, Berlin.

The movement soon spread to Austria-Hungary, where it
was fanned by idiotic charges that Jews in the town of Tisza-
Eszlar had murdered a Christian child in order to use his
blood for their rituals. In 1882 the first of a series of anti-
Semitic congresses was held in Dresden, where fantastically
medieval restrictions were demanded against the Jews.

Even France felt the wave of hatred. And again, a financial
collapse provided the spur. It seemed that certain Catholic
bankers and aristocrats had decided to invest in a banking
organization known as the Union Générale, with the idea of
putting the Rothschilds out of business. The Union Générale
failed catastrophically, and a lot of influential people lost a lot

of money. The usual scapegoat was at hand, however. Edouard Drumont wrote a venomously anti-Semitic book entitled *La France juive* (*Jewish France*) in 1886 to prove that everything bad which had ever happened in France was the result of Jewish conspiracies and machinations. It was one of the most popular books of the century. Matters came to a head in 1894 when Captain Alfred Dreyfus, a member of the French General Staff, was accused of betraying French military secrets to the German government. Dreyfus was innocent — but Dreyfus was a Jew. To the accompaniment of a wild anti-Jewish campaign in the press, he was sentenced to life imprisonment on Devil's Island.

Subsequently it was found that the evidence against Dreyfus had been forged. Furthermore, it was obvious that the whole affair was part of a plot against the very existence of the French Republic by royalists, anti-Semites, and Catholic bigots. Liberal Frenchmen, led by the novelists Emile Zola and Anatole France, waged a campaign to awaken their countrymen's conscience. Soon the country was divided into two camps. Dreyfus was recalled from Devil's Island, tried again, and again found guilty — on patently false evidence after a totally unfair trial. The president of France, appalled by the results, gave Dreyfus a free pardon and, later, the French court of appeals proclaimed him an innocent man. But in the meantime half of France had revealed itself as desperately anti-Jewish.

It was very obvious that the reactionaries in Germany and the royalists in France had definite political goals (the destruction of democratic government in their respective countries) which they hoped to achieve through their anti-Semitic campaigns. But those campaigns would have amounted to nothing without popular support. How was it that at the end of the nineteenth century, vast masses of supposedly educated Europeans could be found to swallow the anti-Semitic lies? Because those masses were desperately poor, desperately exploited, desperately miserable in their daily lives. The great hopes awakened by the industrial revolution, by the advent of capitalism and democracy, had not been realized. Conditions of life for most Europeans had not changed. Somehow the "modern" world was going wrong — and there had to be a reason. Socialists and labor leaders were accusing the new ruling classes of hoarding the wealth created by industrialization; sometimes they accused the entire capitalist system. Under attack, those same ruling classes discovered in the new anti-Semitism a means of diverting popular wrath from themselves. Their hired propagandists (themselves self-convinced fanatics) offered the eternal scapegoat — the Jew — as a lightning rod for popular discontent. And two thousand years of religious propaganda, segregation, and traditional hatred bred into Christian European culture made their task easier. It is notable that those sections of the working class imbued with or inspired by socialist ideals rejected the new anti-Semitism. It found its true support among unorganized labor, in the peasantry (where it had always existed) and, above all, in the lower middle class — the small shopkeepers, independent farmers, and tradespeople, whose precarious position in the new capitalist society kept them in a constant state of fear and impotent rage.

In western Europe in the late nineteenth century anti-Semitism drew little blood, aside from the occasional outbreak of riots in Germany or Austria-Hungary. But in the east it had far different consequences. On the thirteenth of March, 1881, the Russian Tsar, Alexander II, was assassinated by a group of student rebels. This event was seized upon by the most reactionary elements in Russia as the pretext for an attack upon those individuals and groups in that semifeudal society who were suspected of liberal leanings. Needless to say, Russian

Jews were among the primary targets. On April 27, 1881, anti-Jewish rioting, inspired by government agents, broke out in the province of Kherson. For two days the fury raged while the police watched impassively. Hundreds of Jews were killed, women were raped, nearly a thousand homes and synagogues were destroyed. And the Kherson example spread like wildfire. There were wholesale massacres at Kiev and Odessa in May. By autumn Jews had been martyred in no less than one hundred and sixty localities in southern Russia. At Christmas, another series of bloody riots broke out in Warsaw, in Russian-ruled Poland, and continued throughout that unhappy land until the summer of 1882.

The rest of Europe stood aghast at this barbarism. A new word entered the English language — *pogrom* (Russian for "devastation") — the term referred to the massacres. In the West it had been thought that the age of savagery was long past — but Russia was not the West. Russia remained frozen in an autocratic, medieval mold. And as the Russian Tsarist government felt itself increasingly threatened by revolutionists — organizing now under the banners of various brands of socialism — it vented its spleen with ever fiercer cruelty upon the six million Jews (by far the largest Jewish community in the world) it held prisoner. Beginning in May, 1882, the Tsar's government began issuing a series of laws which finally reimposed completely medieval restrictions upon Jews. They were forbidden to enter various trades, professions, and educational institutions; they were forbidden to reside in villages or in the countryside; they were forbidden to live anywhere outside certain areas of Poland (called the Pale of Settlement) — and the new laws were enforced with ferocious severity. Thus, in 1891, thousands of Jews were driven from Moscow in midwinter to make their way through the blizzards to Poland. In 1898 seven thousand were driven from Kiev. It was no matter of wonder that so many of the Russian revolutionists (the most important being Leon Trotsky, born Lev Bronstein) were Jewish.

In 1905, following Russian defeat in the Russo-Japanese
War, revolution broke out throughout the Russian Empire. A
constitution of sorts was forced upon the Tsar and it provided
for some amelioration of the conditions under which Russian
Jews lived. But this constitution was speedily swept aside when
the Tsar regained control of the principal cities — and
pogroms were launched against Jewish communities everywhere. These were carried out now by the Tsarist secret
organizations known as the Black Hundreds, which received
governmental support and protection. Within four years of
the collapse of the Revolution of 1905 no fewer than two hundred and eighty-four cities and towns were swept by pogroms
— and more than fifty thousand Jews were killed in circumstances of the utmost cruelty. Jewish life in eastern Europe
became a prolonged nightmare.

One result of this new martyrdom was the flight of Polish
and Russian Jews to the West. By the thousands, the tens of
thousands, the hundreds of thousands, they sought refuge
wherever they could: in neighboring Germany and Austria-
Hungary (where the new anti-Semitism made them unwelcome guests), in France and the Low Countries — but most of
all, in England and the United States, where anti-Semitism was
not, at least, a life-and-death matter and where economic
opportunity beckoned. In London the Jewish population
jumped from 47,000 to 150,000 in the space of a single decade;
throughout England Jewish communities expanded and new
ones were formed. But it was the United States, the land of
opportunity — a land dreamed of almost as a new Zion by the
oppressed Jews — which received the greatest influx. Between
1881 and 1900 more than 600,000 eastern European Jews
landed at American ports. By 1906 another half million ar-

rived. By 1929 the total had risen to over 2,300,000, of whom
71 percent were Russian. In the course of a single generation,
one third of all eastern European Jews had crossed the ocean
to start a new life in the New World. In 1870 there had been
fewer than 250,000 Jews in the United States — by 1930 there
were more than four million.

The new arrivals naturally tended to settle in New York,
the principal port of entry. They seldom had enough money to
penetrate farther into the country, and besides, New York was
the urban and manufacturing center of the nation, where jobs
were easiest to come by. By 1930 there were no fewer than
1,750,000 Jews living in New York — one third of the city's
population. At no other time in five thousand years of history
had so many Jews ever been gathered together in one place.

The eastern European Jews brought with them their traditional skills. They entered the tailoring trade, clothing manufacturing, cabinetmaking, tobacco-working, the fur industry,
and similar callings. They created newspapers, theaters, and
two of the strongest and most militant trades unions in the
country — the Amalgamated Clothing Workers of America
and the International Ladies Garment Workers Union.
Within a generation there were Jewish doctors, lawyers,
mechanics, printers, and even farmers — all merging into
American life. The East Side of New York became a vast melting pot into which all sorts and conditions of men were
poured, tried, and molded. From it emerged history's largest
and strongest Jewish community — one which would deeply
influence the destinies of the land of its adoption.

Another result of the eastern European martyrdom and the
renewal of anti-Semitism in western Europe was the rebirth of
the ancient dream of a Jewish national homeland. Assimilation, except in England and the United States, was, it seemed,
an illusory goal. After a century of liberal dreaming, the Jews

of western Europe were awakening to the fact that the ancient hatreds had never really died — and the fate of Russian Jews was a cruel example of what the future anywhere might hold for them. A prophet of this awakening was Moses Hess.

Born in the Rhineland in 1812, Hess grew up into the world of German revolutionary theory and socialist thought. Although a friend and collaborator of Karl Marx, Hess, unlike Marx, had been raised an orthodox Jew — he spoke Yiddish before he spoke German. And while Hess, in his early years, mouthed all the correct socialist views on the "Jewish Question" (mainly that it would "go away" once a socialist order was established), he could never really convince himself that Jews were simply an economic category rather than a distinct people. Perhaps because his mother was Polish and, unlike other western European Jewish intellectuals, he knew the extreme poverty and despair of the Jews of eastern Europe, Hess was able to avoid the Marxist stereotypes. To Hess, the Jews, like the Marxist proletariat, were an oppressed people, scattered among the nations. And like the proletariat, this oppressed people bore a historical mission of redemption for all mankind.

After the collapse of the revolutionary movements of 1848, Moses Hess settled in Paris, where he reflected deeply on the destiny of his people. The hope of a national restoration to Palestine — the dream of Zion — was central not only to Jewish experience, but also to Jewish religious belief. Hess himself, as a good socialist, was an opponent of organized religion. But he could never equate the established national churches such as the Catholic Church in France or the Lutheran Church in Prussia with the religious and cultural heritage of an oppressed minority people. Did emancipation require that Jews give up the hope of Zion? If so, Hess advised his generation to reject emancipation as not worth the price. Jewish national restoration was a necessity, he declared, not only for Jews, but for the world. Everywhere liberals were hailing the right of nations to a free life of their own. If the Italians (then engaged in their wars of national unification) were entitled to national freedom, why not the Jews? If the liberation of Rome was an act of historic justice, why not the liberation of Jerusalem?

Hess embodied his thoughts on this subject in a slim book called *Rome and Jerusalem, the Latest National Question*, published in Leipzig in 1862. It was philosophical, theoretical, and very rational. But it was neither a practical guide nor a clarion call to action. When the book appeared it received scant attention — except for the derision of various assimilationist Jews to whom the entire idea of a Jewish national state was hateful. Moses Hess died in Paris in 1875 and was buried in Cologne. His writings, however, outlived him — today they are Zionist classics.

If disillusionment with both emancipation and the promise of socialism stung Moses Hess into a new dream of Zion, the bloody pogroms of Tsarist Russia awakened the Jews of eastern Europe. Reeling from the terrible riots of 1881, Jews in Russia, Poland, and Romania began forming self-help societies in several cities. The movement was named *Chibat Zion* (Love of Zion) and its adherents called themselves *Chovevei Zion* (Lovers of Zion). Since it was perfectly obvious that there could be no emancipation in a society where hatred of the Jews was fostered by government policy, the self-help societies could hope only for escape. They could not dream of the practical, but only of the impossible — the restoration of a Jewish national state in Palestine to which they might flee. And in 1882, armed only with faith and desperation, a handful of ex-university students (they numbered twenty) set out for the Holy Land. They were known as *Biluim* (the plural of a

name compounded of the initials of the Hebrew words meaning "House of Jacob, come and let us go"), and they were to
be the shock troops of the First Aliyah (the first "Going Up"
— or "Wave").

In 1884 thirty-four delegates from most of the Chovevei
Zion societies in Russia, Romania, and Galicia (then part of
Austria-Hungary) met to confer in the city of Kattowitz in
German Silesia (such a meeting held in Russia would have
been an invitation to massacre). There they federated and
chose for their president an elderly physician named Leon
Pinsker.

Pinsker had, for most of his life, trod the path of emancipation. He had drunk deep at the fount of "enlightenment," had
been known as a "Russianizer," one who urged his fellow Jews
to assimilate into their societies. But the bloody massacres of
1881 opened his eyes. Although Pinsker was a man of unblem-
ished character, courage and lofty idealism, he owes his place
in the story of Zionism not to his presidency of Chibat Zion,
but rather to a pamphlet he had written two years before,
entitled *Auto-Emancipation*.

In this work, Pinsker probed into the cancer of anti-
Semitism and proclaimed it incurable. It was a morbid dread
of something strange and mysterious, he declared: "the ghost-
like apparition of a people without . . . land or other bond of
union, no longer alive and yet moving about among the living." It was not only that the nations of the world regarded the
Jews as strangers — after all, nations were accustomed to seeing
people of other nationalities living among them. But while
these others could be identified with some definite people and
land somewhere on the face of the earth, the Jews could not.
The strangeness of the Jews was unique and disturbing; the
fears and hatreds it aroused would not yield to reason. "Prejudice, or intuitive ill-will," declared Pinsker, "can be satisfied

by no reasoning, however forceful or clear." Nor would it be cured by the progress of "enlightenment." The only remedy was "the creation of a Jewish nationality . . . living on its own soil." Pinsker did not, in this pamphlet, insist that Palestine itself must be the site of the new Jewish nation, but in 1883 he wrote: "Let us obtain dry bread by the sweat of our brow on the sacred soil of our ancestors."

By its very title, *Auto-Emancipation* challenged the assimilationists. It summoned Jews everywhere to stand up and emancipate themselves. And it was to have a deep impact on the next generation of Jews.

The Kattowitz conference adopted as the overall name for the new federation of Chovevei Zion societies, *Mazkeret Moshe* (Souvenir of Moses). This quaint title was not chosen, however, to honor the great lawgiver of the Bible, but rather to lure the support of the famous French financier and Jewish philanthropist, Moses Montefiore (then one hundred years old). Montefiore was touched by the honor, but his advisors felt that the new federation was dangerously political in flavor. Therefore its name was changed to "The Montefiore Association for the Promotion of Agriculture among Jews and Especially for the Support of the Jewish Colonies in Palestine." It was thought that so long, involved, and obscure a name might not draw down too much Tsarist wrath. The federation established headquarters in Odessa on the Black Sea and, after prolonged wrangles with the Russian government, obtained recognition. It did not, however, obtain much money — the sums it forwarded to Palestine were always pitifully insufficient to meet the needs of the colonizers there. The "Odessa Committee," as it came to be known, lasted until 1919, when the new Bolshevik Russian government put an end to it.

Chovevei Zion won support throughout western Europe and the United States — but also found opposition. In America, many, if not most, Jews felt they had already found their Promised Land. Most of the supporters of the movement in the United States were those refugee Russian Jews who had experienced at first hand the terrors of the pogroms. Nonetheless Chovevei Zion earned the very influential support of certain American Jews, especially Rabbi Aaron Wise of Temple Rodeph Shalom in New York, whose son Stephen was one day to play a great role in Zionism. And this was, in a sense, the most important accomplishment of Chovevei Zion — it prepared the way, intellectually and practically, for a Zionist future.

Meanwhile, what of the first settlers who had gone out to Palestine in 1882? When the Biluim arrived there were already about twenty-five thousand Jews in Palestine — for the most part descendants of those who had found refuge under the Turkish sultans during the great expulsions from Spain and Portugal. Nearly all of these Palestinian Jews lived in the "four Holy Cities": Safed, Hebron, Tiberius, and Jerusalem. These communities were almost completely dependent for their daily bread upon the charity of Jews living all over the world — a charity which the Biluim felt led only to stagnation. For the "shock troops" of the First Aliyah came to Palestine not only with courage, but also with an ideology. Basic to their outlook was the conviction that the life of the redeemed nation must rest upon productive labor and a return to the soil. Furthermore, the agricultural life of the state must be cooperative and express the principles of social justice, "for that is the function of Israel in the land of Israel, the land of the prophets." Before they landed in Jaffa harbor on August 11, 1882, the Biluim wrote down their hopes, dreams, principles, and obligations in a kind of latter-day "Mayflower Compact," partly inspired by the first.

For most of the next decade these young idealists suffered

privation, anguish, hunger, sickness, and neglect. Their only equipment was passionate belief in the future of Israel — everything else they lacked. They had no money, no training in agriculture, no experience of physical labor. They had to face the hostility of Turkish government officials and Arab neighbors, as well as the indifference of the older Jewish communities in Palestine. After two years of toiling, the new pioneers found a patron in the person of Yechiel Pines, a Palestinian Jew who bought a piece of land between Jaffa and Gaza on which the Biluim could settle. They named their colony Gederah (Rampart), but for years it proved no rampart against distress. "We shall never forget the past winter because of the hunger we endured," wrote Chaim Chissin, one of the settlers. "We did not even eat our fill of dry bread. As for a cup of tea or a spoonful of soup, such luxuries we could allow ourselves only on rare occasions." They were often on the brink of despair, but never quite succumbed. With a little help from the Odessa Committee they maintained themselves and even began to forge ahead. Then, in the early winter of 1889 a large band of Arabs from neighboring villages attacked Gederah. The battle lasted for three days — a battle of bullets and stones — before the Arabs finally drew off. Gederah was saved, but remained on the edge of extinction.

By that time there were other little settlements in Palestine; Rishon Lezion (First in Zion), Ekron, Ness Ziona, and others. All were agricultural communities and all, by 1889, faced defeat. The settlements were saved by the princely generosity of a single man, Baron Edmund de Rothschild of Paris. He spent more than £5 million (equivalent today to much more than $100 million) helping the Jewish settlements and earned for himself the title of "Father of the Jewish Community of Palestine." Along with his money, Baron Rothschild sent expert agronomists and administrators to Palestine. They changed the emphasis of agriculture from grain-growing (for which there was insufficient land) to vineyards, which soon proved successful. But the baron shrank from mass movements and political programs. His administrators did not share the Chovevei Zion dream of a new national state in Palestine — they were simply engaged in a work of constructive philanthropy, and the result was a kind of paternalism which devitalized the larger goal.

But the spirit of the colonists was being eroded by more than paternalism. The Jewish colonists from eastern Europe had no experience of manual labor and no knowledge of agriculture. The actual hard work in the settlements was too often being done by hired Arabs, and not by Jews. The children of the colonists were growing up with little attachment to the land. Philanthropy and cheap native labor was the way of imperialism — not the way to restore a people to its land. And, worst of all, the entire structure of Jewish resettlement in Palestine had no legal foundation in Turkish law. It was accomplished by bribing local Turkish officials. In 1891, after a severe Russian pogrom, a fresh wave of immigrants arrived. The port city of Jaffa took on the look of a boom town. Great plans were made for expansion of the Jewish settlements — and then the bubble burst. The Turkish government became alarmed at this sudden growth. Overnight a new edict went forth: the sale of land to Jews was prohibited, and further Jewish immigration was drastically curtailed. The precariousness of the Jewish position in Palestine was suddenly and glaringly revealed.

Among the "Lovers of Zion" the conviction grew that the great dream of regaining a national homeland could not be achieved on the road they were following. Israel would not be restored by private philanthropy, bribes and catering to the whims of the decadent Turkish regime. Something greater was needed — a new vision, perhaps a new visionary.

Haggada:

Christian Voices

"I really wish the Jews again in Judea an independent nation . . . [which] may be admitted to all the privileges of citizens in every part of the world."

> — *John Adams (1819)*

"I cannot conceal from you my most anxious desire to see your countrymen endeavour once more to resume their existence as a people."

> — *Colonel Henry Churchill (to Moses Montefiore, 1840)*

"There is a store of wisdom among us to found a new Jewish polity, grand, simple, just, like the old. . . . Then our race shall have an organic center, a heart and brain to watch and guide and execute; the outraged Jew shall have a defence in the court of nations, as the outraged Englishman or American. And the world will gain as Israel gains. For there will be a community in the van of the East which carries the culture and sympathies

of every great nation in its bosom; and there will be a land set
for the halting place of enmities, a neutral ground for the East
as Belgium is for the West. Difficulties? I know there are difficulties. But let the spirit of divine achievement move in the
great among our people and the work will begin. . . . Let the
central fire be kindled again, and the light will reach afar. . . .
The Messianic time is the time when Israel shall will the
planting of the national Ensign. . . . The Vision is there: it will
be fulfilled."

— *George Eliot,* Daniel
Deronda, *1876*

"What shall be done for the Russian Jews? . . . Why not give
Palestine back to them again? . . . Under their cultivation it
was a remarkably fruitful land, sustaining millions of Israelites
who industriously tilled its hillsides and valleys. . . . A million
of exiles by their terrible sufferings are piteously appealing to
our sympathy, justice and humanity. . . ."

— *Reverend William E.
Blackstone, in a me-
morial to President
Benjamin Harrison,
1891. (Among the hun-
dreds of leaders of
American opinion who
signed this memorial
were J. Pierpont Mor-
gan, John D. Rockefel-
ler, Cyrus W. Field,
Philip D. Armour, and
William E. Dodge.)*

6

A Dream in Search of Reality

And what glory awaits those who fight unselfishly for the
cause! Therefore I believe that a wonderful generation of
Jews will spring into existence. The Maccabees will rise again.
Let me once more repeat my opening words: The Jews who
will it shall have a state of their own.

THEODOR HERZL

The visionary who was to become the father of the modern
Zionist movement was born in the year 1860 in Budapest, then
the capitol of the Hungarian part of the Austro-Hungarian
Empire. In 1878 when Theodor Herzl (his Hebrew name
was Benjamin Zeev) was eighteen years old, his family moved
to the imperial capital, Vienna — and it was that city which
left the deepest impression on his youth. His early life was
filled with the romantic hopes and frustrations of a generation
of Viennese Jewish intellectuals who were caught between the
sentimental fantasies of a declining aristocratic society and a
thoroughly anti-Semitic people. Technically, the Jews of
Austria-Hungary had been granted full civil equality in 1867,
but large sectors of social and economic life remained closed to
them. For example, although Theodor Herzl received a doc-
torate of Laws from the University of Vienna in 1884, he
could not hope to advance himself to any notable position in
government. He could not, in fact, hope to find any clients at
all, except from the world of Jewish finance — a world which
he, like most of his friends, scorned as unworthy. But it was the

persistence of these hidden barriers to full Jewish participation in the life of the nation which preserved in Herzl's generation a Jewish identity which they might otherwise have given up in the sea of assimilation.

In Herzl's day the Jewish population of Vienna was a whole world in itself, large, lively and imbued with the hopes of liberalism. It was rich in artists and intellectuals, in writers, poets, and philosophers. While the older generation of Jews, the generation of the emancipation, still cherished the liberal dreams, many of the younger generation now looked to socialism as the path to complete freedom. But whatever their political persuasion, all Viennese Jews shared the nineteenth century's deep and abiding faith in rationality: all problems would eventually be solved by man's mind — if only man willed it so. Herzl himself became a socialist — but not a very active one, since his life remained comfortable within its limits.

Not that he had no firsthand experience of the new anti-Semitism. Once in his early teens (as he tells us in his voluminous *Diaries*) he had been deeply hurt when one of his teachers defined the word "heathen" as including "idolators, Mohammedans and Jews." In 1881, while attending the university, he had come across a book by the German anti-Semite Eugene Duhring entitled *The Jewish Problem as a Problem of Race, Morals and Culture* — one of the best-sellers of its day. The book both offended and frightened Herzl, who still thought that the "Jewish Question" would disappear with assimilation. If so prominent an author as Duhring entertained such dismally prejudiced views of the Jews, "What are we to expect from the ignorant masses?" Herzl asked his diary. And again, in 1883, his student fraternity (a club composed mostly of elegant young aristocrats) took part in an anti-Semitic demonstration. Young Herzl immediately resigned. "It must be clear to every decent person," he wrote to the fraternity, "that under these circumstances, I cannot wish to retain my membership."

It was not as a lawyer that young Herzl first found success, but as a writer. His plays were produced in Vienna, Berlin, and Prague, and his brilliant essays were published in many newspapers. In 1891 he received the prize that he coveted most: the large and influential Jewish-owned *Neue Freie Presse* of Vienna, one of the capital's leading liberal newspapers, made him their Paris correspondent.

In the Paris of the early 1890s the atmosphere was more relaxed than in anti-Semitic Vienna. There, Herzl thought, he could forget about the "Jewish Question." But he was deluding himself. He was not a man in whom the sense of injustice could be quelled. He felt he owed something to his Jewishness, that he had to face the rising tide of anti-Semitism. He did so in a play written in 1894 entitled *The New Ghetto*. It is the story of a young, emancipated Jew who is frustrated, tormented, and finally destroyed by the new society which has admitted him without accepting him. "I have written it for a nation of anti-Semites," he wrote to his friend Arthur Schnitzler in Vienna. "The play must be produced! It must speak from the stage! If this play reaches the world it will be my release." Three years later *The New Ghetto* was, in fact, produced — but not with the results for which Herzl had hoped. In the meantime a great wave of anti-Semitism had arisen in France.

Just after Herzl had written *The New Ghetto*, the Dreyfus case exploded like a bombshell in Paris. As a newspaper correspondent Herzl witnessed the grim ceremony enacted on January 5, 1895, on the parade grounds of the Ecole Militaire, where, in the presence of his brother officers and five thousand troops drawn up in stiff formation, Captain Dreyfus was degraded — the insignia torn from his uniform, his sword broken. And Herzl heard Dreyfus cry out repeatedly "I am innocent!" He also heard the responding growl from the huge crowd of civilian onlookers, "Death to the Jews!" Although Herzl felt that Dreyfus was innocent, what really shocked him was the ugly anti-Semitism of the mob, and the fact that the incident had occurred in Paris — the home of that very revolution which had brought about Jewish emancipation. The spectacle of Dreyfus's degradation stunned Herzl into his life's work. To his diary he confided (in June, 1895): "For some time I have been engaged in a work. . . . It has the appearance of a stupendous dream, but for days and weeks it has absorbed me to the point of unconsciousness. It accompanies me wherever I go . . . haunts and intoxicates me." The work, which was published in Vienna in February, 1896, was a short book entitled *Der Judenstaat* (*The Jewish State*). Its appearance marks the beginning of Zionism as a viable idea — something more than a dream.

What is remarkable about *Der Judenstaat* is Herzl's self-control, his statesmanlike approach to a problem that tormented him personally. He deals very reasonably and rationally with that vexed and grievous eternal "Jewish Problem," dissects the new anti-Semitism without fear or mercy, and coldly appraises the frightening prospects facing the Jews. "We are a people — one people," he states, and adds, "a people that will not be left in peace." In a single sentence he sums up his proposed solution: "Let the sovereignty be granted us over a portion of the globe large enough to satisfy the rightful requirements of a nation; the rest we shall manage for ourselves." It is notable that he does not here insist that Palestine shall be that "portion of the globe" — that would come to him later.

Herzl not only issued a clarion call in *Der Judenstaat* — he went into some detail about the Jewish state he envisioned. First of all, it would be necessary to create a "Society of Jews" which could be publicly and legally recognized as the political representative of the Jewish people. Then a "Jewish Company" would be founded to serve as the financial and executive agent of the society. The "grant" of "sovereignty" would be made to the society with the approval of the European powers. This "grant" would later be designated a "charter" — the illusive pursuit of which would consume the rest of Herzl's life. The operations of the Jewish company which would actually direct the colonization were clearly outlined — how it would raise money, promote agriculture and industry, protect labor, and encourage emigration to the new state. He pointed out that "great exertions will hardly be necessary to spur on the Movement; anti-Semites will provide the requisite impetus." In conclusion he exhorted to action: "It has never yet been possible: now it is possible! . . . We shall live at last as free men on our own soil, and die peacefully in our own homes. The world will be liberated by our freedom, enriched by our wealth, magnified by our greatness. And whatever we attempt to accomplish for our own welfare, will react powerfully and beneficently for the good of humanity."

In his preface to *Der Judenstaat* Herzl wrote: "I feel that with the publication of this pamphlet, my task is done." But he was wrong — his task had only just begun. In fact, he had begun it even before writing *Der Judenstaat*. He had tried to enlist the support of the wealthiest men in France for his enterprise. He had approached both Edmund de Rothschild and Baron Maurice de Hirsch. Rothschild refused to see him, while Hirsch simply said "Fantastic," when he heard Herzl's scheme and then dismissed the matter from his mind. No doubt both these philanthropists considered Herzl's idea too dangerously political.

The reception that *Der Judenstaat* met among Jewish leaders in western Europe ranged at first from anger to laughter.

Anger that any Jew would dare to raise his voice in such a way
as to threaten the very delicate balance upon which emancipated Jews lived. Laughter at the crazy idea that a state, a
nation, could be brought into being simply because a mass of
powerless people willed it. Even in eastern Europe the book
was greeted with misgivings — largely because it made no ref-
erence whatsoever to the work of Pinsker and the Chovevei
Zion societies. Furthermore, if Herzl meant to create a state in
Palestine, this might well arouse the wrath of the Turkish
government, upon whose slumberous corruption the infant
settlements in Palestine depended for their continued existence.

But the doubts and misgivings expressed by Jewish leaders
west and east were not shared by their followers. There was
that in *Der Judenstaat* which touched the deepest longings
and aspirations of Jews everywhere. In Russia, Romania, England, Austria-Hungary, France — everywhere the Chovevei
Zion societies, synagogue congregations, student groups passed
resolutions and organized petitions bearing thousands of signa-
tures in support of Herzl's goals. Without himself willing it, or
even wanting it, Herzl was propelled into a position of leadership.

Still he tried to "arrange" matters at the top. He conceived
the idea that a group of the wealthiest Jews in Europe would
arrange for the payment and funding of the Turkish national
debt. In return for that, the sultan would grant the Jews a
charter to settle and govern Palestine. This plan was not so
wild as it may appear today. The Turkish national debt was
well within the capacity of the Rothschilds, Hirsches, Péreires,
and others to handle — and the sultan was corrupt enough to
sell a part of his empire. But despite the fact that Herzl enlisted the verbal support of Wilhelm II, Emperor of Germany,
and King Ferdinand of Bulgaria, he could not win adherents

among wealthy Jews. They felt that to meddle in high politics in this way was simply to invite trouble. The prospects of achieving his goal by starting at the top vanished. The only way was by organizing the masses. For somewhere it had been decreed that Zionism was to be more than a financial and diplomatic enterprise — it was to be the deep surge of an ancient and long-suffering people.

Early in March, 1897, Herzl and a few of his more devoted followers in Vienna issued a call for a general congress of Zionists of every persuasion to meet in Munich, Germany. When the leaders of the Munich Jewish community, fearing an anti-Semitic backlash, protested against this, the meeting was transferred to Basel, Switzerland. There on August 29, 1897, the First Zionist Congress was opened. Two hundred and four delegates, hailing from every nation and from Palestine itself, attended. There were old and young, students and bearded rabbis, bourgeois and socialists, Orthodox and Reformed — speaking dozens of languages, united only in their Jewishness. Could this motley group be welded into a single disciplined organization?

They could. In three days of speeches, reports and meetings, the Zionist Congress elected Herzl its president, adopted a platform, and created a new entity, the World Zionist Organization, to further its aims. Those aims were declared to be "to create a publicly recognized, legally secured home for the Jewish people in Palestine." The new organization was to be open to all who supported its goals. Local and national organizations were to be created which would in turn elect delegates to the world congresses, which would be held yearly. Everything was arranged according to the most democratic principles. And the First Congress also adopted a song and a flag. The song was "Hatikvah" ("The Hope"). Its words were written by a Hebrew poet named Naphtali Herz Imber, its melody drawn from an ancient, haunting refrain of unknown authorship. The design for the flag — broad stripes of blue and white with a blue Star of David in its center — is attributed to David Wolffsohn (one of Herzl's most zealous supporters in Vienna). Wolffsohn's design was probably inspired by the traditional Jewish prayer shawl.

The effect of this First Congress, both upon those who attended it and those who heard its echoes, was magical. For the first time since the Romans had destroyed the Jewish state, a long-dispersed people had gathered together again through their representatives and set themselves a transcendent goal. Herzl later wrote in his diary: "In Basel I founded the Jewish State." He was right. For, as David Ben-Gurion, the first prime minister of the State of Israel, was to observe fifty years later, "On that day the Jewish State was indeed founded, for a state is founded first in the hearts of the people."

When the delegates to the First Zionist Congress returned to their homes in many countries, they brought with them a spark from the central fire. And the sparks burst into flame. Within one year of the Basel Conference there were no fewer than 913 Zionist societies scattered around the world, from Russian villages to great American cities. Everywhere the poor and humble flocked to the new standard, contributing their pennies, inspired by a new dream. There was also opposition — not merely the ridicule of anti-Semites, but opposition among some Jews. This opposition had two main centers. One was the Jewish socialist movement represented by the *Bund* (Alliance), as the "General Jewish Workers' Alliance of Lithuania, Poland and Russia" was called. The Bund, which, like other Marxist-inspired Russian parties, could see salvation only in a revolution against the dreadful Tsarist autocracy, held the view that Zionism was reactionary. Jews should stay where they were and join the class struggle. For only through the international socialist revolution (always just around the corner) could mankind's problems be solved — and with them, the problems of the Jews. The other pole of anti-Zionism among Jews was that represented by the very rich, assimilated Jews of western Europe: the Rothschilds, the Péreires, Hirsches, and so on. These men of high finance well knew how recent and precarious was their rise to prosperity and "acceptance." While they were willing to pour out millions in charity to their less fortunate fellow Jews, they felt that Zionism made all Jews into "high profile" targets. They wanted the world to forget about Jews — that way lay salvation. Also, the political implications of Zionism, which, after all, involved a dismemberment of the Ottoman Empire, embarrassed them.

Nevertheless, Herzl threw himself heart and soul into the new work — with inextinguishable optimism. He was the editor of the movement's central newspaper in Vienna, *Die Welt* (*The World*), and kept it going with his own money. He wrote, traveled, argued, and fought for his dream. "I am tired and my heart is not in good order," he notes in his diary. And later: "I am still fighting with a wooden sword when I need a sword of steel." And still later: "We are still like the soldiers of the French Revolution. We must go barefoot into battle."

Within months of the First Congress, Herzl thought he saw a golden opportunity. It seemed that Kaiser Wilhelm II of Germany was about to pay a state visit to the Sultan of Turkey in Constantinople. Later the German emperor would visit Jerusalem. This was, of course, because the Kaiser was anxious to extend German "influence" over the Ottoman Empire — but Zionists welcomed such a move. At the close of the nineteenth century Turkey, debt-ridden, corrupt and weak, despite its extensive Near Eastern empire, was known as "The sick man of Europe." The Kaiser, on the other hand, was not yet widely perceived as the sword-rattling idiot whose bombast and ambitions would one day help plunge mankind into the horrors of the First World War. It might be possible to reason with the Kaiser — and he in turn could exert a powerful and civilized influence over the decadent sultan. The proposition remained the same: Jews would "fund" the Turkish national debt if the sultan would issue a charter that gave them freedom to settle in Palestine.

Herzl wangled an interview with the Kaiser in Constantinople and on October 18, 1898, the meeting took place. It was fabulous. Here was a man armed only with a dream coming to negotiate with the ruler of a great empire — and yet the interview went quite well. Wilhelm was young enough and arrogant enough to envision himself as a "protector" of the Jews — just as he wished to "protect" so many other peoples. He assured Herzl that he would win the approval of the sultan for the project — and matters would be concluded at a second meeting in Jerusalem itself. Herzl set off exultantly for Palestine to await the Kaiser's arrival.

This was to be Herzl's one and only visit to Zion. On the way from the port of Jaffa to Jerusalem, he and his party were hailed in all the little Jewish Chovevei Zion settlements. But Herzl detected the paralyzing hand of paternalism in those places. As for the Holy City itself, he found it an enchantment by moonlight, but a depressing sink of poverty, congestion, and filth by day. "The day the city is ours," he noted in his diary, "and I am still alive and able, my first act will be to cleanse thee, O Jerusalem!"

On November 2, 1898, Kaiser Wilhelm entered Jerusalem (a large hole being knocked out of the walls enclosing the Jaffa Gate so that the monarch might enter astride a white charger) and met with Herzl that same day. But this second meeting proved a disappointment. While the Kaiser may have toyed with the idea of entering history as a second Moses (and hoped that Zionism might relieve him of his unwelcome Jew-ish population in Germany), it was very obvious that his advisors — hardened anti-Semites all — had little sympathy for Jewish hopes. Furthermore, the sultan had evidently not been so easily "influenced" by his new friend. Wilhelm responded to Herzl's pleas with vague evasions and trivial nonsense. "Yes," he observed pompously, "the soil is cultivable; what the country needs is shade and water; your movement is based on a sound idea." Herzl soon realized that he had reached a dead end.

Herzl returned to Vienna and his labors. A second and third Zionist congress were held and the movement showed growth and vitality — among the poor of all lands, if not among the wealthy magnates.

The Fourth Congress was held in London, for Herzl had abandoned hope of German support and concluded that Zion-ism must orient itself toward Great Britain. "England the great, England the free," he exclaimed, "England with her eyes scanning the seven seas, will understand us. From this place the Zionist Movement will rise to new heights!" No more prophetic words were ever uttered.

Eight months later Herzl finally had his long-sought inter-view with "the skinny little man with the big crooked nose and dyed beard," His Imperial Majesty Abdul-Hamid Khan II, Sultan of Turkey and ruler of the Ottoman Empire. The sultan and his ministers, all of whom had their hands out for bribes, were intrigued by Herzl's offer — two million pounds sterling for a charter. But the eely, slippery intrigues of the court at Constantinople were such that nothing would be promised — only hinted at. Let the Jews come up with their two million pounds, then the sultan would further consider the matter — favorably, favorably. Herzl sped off to Paris and London. Surely now, with this literally golden opportunity before them, the rich Jews would be forthcoming. But they were not. "There will have to be a flood of fire and brimstone before those stones will soften up," Herzl bitterly observed. A little later a group of French financiers persuaded the sultan to accept their own money at very high rates of interest — and the deal was off. "I expected the Sultan would not let me leave empty-handed, but matters turned out otherwise," Herzl confided to his diary. "With him things always turn out in a way one does not expect. Perhaps at an unforeseen moment, I shall obtain the Charter from him. And perhaps not from him at all, for it is possible that we shall obtain the Charter only after the partition of Turkey by the Powers."

Meanwhile a new avenue of hope opened in London. The terrible pogroms in eastern Europe had loosed a flood of Jewish refugees into England, and a Royal Commission on Alien Immigration was holding hearings on the matter — with a view to cutting off the tide. Herzl appeared to testify before this commission and, later, through the good offices of Nathaniel, first Lord Rothschild, gained an audience with the English Colonial Secretary, Joseph Chamberlain, and the Foreign Secretary, Lord Lansdowne. In brief, Herzl proposed that if the British government would not support Zionist pretensions in Palestine, perhaps they might allow Jews to settle in Cyprus or the Egyptian Sinai Peninsula. After extensive investigations and negotiations it appeared that neither of these places would be suitable for Jewish immigration. But in 1903, spurred on by new horrors in Russia, the English Colonial Secretary came up with a new idea. Why should not the Jews settle in British East Africa, in a place called Uganda? The British government officially offered this region to the Zionist movement in August, 1903 — and unwittingly started a struggle within Zionism that nearly wrecked the entire movement.

The summation of this controversy had been made even before Britain's proposal became official. The man who made the summation was Dr. Chaim Weizmann, a young (he was then thirty-two) Russian refugee chemist, who was then teaching his subject at Victoria University in Manchester. In the spring of 1903, in the midst of a hard-fought election campaign, British Prime Minister Arthur Balfour came to Manchester. Very much a friend and admirer of the Jews, Balfour had once observed: ". . . Christian religion and civilization owes to Judaism an immeasurable debt, shamefully ill repaid." Before officially making the Uganda proposal to the Zionist organization, Balfour wanted to "try out" the idea on a Zionist. Through a friend, he invited Dr. Weizmann to a fifteen-minute interview — which stretched into more than an hour. Weizmann was terribly nervous at the prospect of explaining to the renowned prime minister in his then-shaky English all the history, dreams, and cross-currents of his people in so short a visit. "I plunged into a long harangue on the meaning of the Zionist Movement," Weizmann later recalled, ". . . that nothing but a deep religious conviction expressed in modern political terms could keep the movement alive and that this conviction had to be based on Palestine and Palestine alone. Any deflection from Palestine was — well, a form of idolatry. . . . I was sweating blood and trying to find some less ponderous way of expressing myself. . . . Suddenly I said: 'Mr. Balfour, supposing I were to offer you Paris instead of London, would you take it?'

"He sat up, looked at me and answered: 'But Dr. Weizmann, we have London.'

" 'That is true,' I said, 'But we had Jerusalem when London was a marsh.' He leaned back and continued to stare at me. . . . I did not see him again until 1914."

Balfour went ahead with the Uganda proposal — but Weizmann had planted a seed that was to bear, in time, a rich harvest.

Herzl himself presented the Uganda proposal to the Sixth Zionist Congress meeting in Basel in August, 1903. Uganda was not and never could be Zion, Herzl admitted, but it might — in Max Nordau's phrase — provide a temporary "shelter for the night." And a dark night it was — for the ferocious pogroms and massacres of Jews in Russia and Poland were then reaching one of their climaxes. Hundreds of thousands wanted to flee but had no place to go. Yet it was the delegates from Russia itself who most bitterly opposed the Uganda scheme. A Zionism without Zion was, they declared, unthinkable. Jewish hearts and minds could not be mobilized to make the sacrifices necessary for success by any other goal than Palestine. The arguments raged fiercely; the votes were close. Delegates were moved to tears and rage. But by a slim majority Herzl retained control over the movement. Yet the debate was not ended with the congress — only started.

Ever optimistic, Herzl continued his labors. He secured an interview with King Victor Emmanuel III of Italy, who expressed his support for Zionism. And while in Rome, Herzl even had an audience with Pope Pius X. But the Supreme Pontiff did not look with favor on the return of Jews to Jerusalem. "If you come to Palestine," the Pope declared, "and settle your people there, we want to have churches and priests ready to baptize you."

In June of 1904 Herzl, suffering from an old heart ailment, went with his wife for a vacation to the little Austrian town of Edlach, near Vienna. There he caught pneumonia. By sheer willpower he kept himself alive until he could see his mother and children again, and then died on the afternoon of July third. "Greet all Palestine for me," he said to a visitor, "and tell them I have given my heart's blood for my people."

Thus ended one of the great lives of modern times. "God breaks the instruments that have served his purpose," Herzl once wrote. And "No Moses ever enters the Promised Land." But in this last prediction he was wrong. For forty-five years later, on August 17, 1949, Herzl's remains were flown in a plane of the Israeli Air Force from Vienna to Tel Aviv, where more than 250,000 men, women and children filed past his coffin as it lay in state outside the Knesset (the Israeli parliament). The following morning it was taken to Jerusalem, where it was buried in a tomb hewn from the rock of Mount Herzl. The mood in Israel that day was not one of sadness, but of solemn joy. Theodor Herzl had come home.

Haggada:

The Sultan and the Dreamer

"[The Sultan] stood before me exactly as I had pictured him; small, thin, with great hooked nose, full dyed beard, a weak quavering voice. . . .

"Then the Sultan said: 'I am and always have been a friend of the Jews. Indeed I rely mainly on the Moslems and Jews. I haven't the same degree of confidence in my other subjects.'

"I thereupon lamented the injustices we experience throughout the world, and he said he had always kept his realm open as an asylum for Jewish refugees.

"At which I said: 'When Professor Vámbéry informed me that His Majesty would receive me, I could not help thinking of the charming old story of Androcles and the lion. His Majesty is the lion, perhaps I am Androcles, and perhaps there is a thorn that needs pulling out.'

"He acknowledged the compliment with a smile.

"Might I speak more openly and to the point? He begged me to do so.

" 'The thorn, as I see it, is your public debt. If that could be removed, the vitality of Turkey, in which I have great faith, would develop new strength.'

"He sighed, and smiled, sighing. . . . His Majesty has concerned himself, ever since he began his glorious reign, with removing this thorn, but in vain. His exalted predecessors had acquired the thorn, and it seems impossible to extract it. If I could do anything about it, it would be more than handsome of me.

" 'Well,' I said, 'I believe I can. But the first and fundamental condition is absolute secrecy.'

"[The Sultan] raised his eyes to heaven, placed his hand upon his breast, and murmured, '*Secret, secret!*' . . .

"I can see him before me now, the Sultan of this declining robber empire. Small, shabby, with his badly dyed beard touched up apparently once a week. . . . The feeble hands in their over-sized gloves . . . the bleating voice, restraint in every word and fear in every glance. And *this* rules!"

> — *Theodor Herzl from*
> The Diaries. *Translation by Marvin Lowenthal*

7

Promises, Promises . . .

> I am persuaded that the Allied Nations, with the fullest con-
> currence of our own government and people, are agreed that
> in Palestine shall be laid the foundations of a Jewish Com-
> monwealth.
>
> WOODROW WILSON

In the years following the death of Theodor Herzl and up to
the First World War, Zionism did not shrink back into the
limited dream of the Chovevei Zion; but neither did it make
any great advance toward its ultimate goals. Nevertheless,
looking back, it can be seen that Zionists settled certain vexing
questions and consolidated their position. They also laid the
groundwork which enabled them to seize hold of opportunity
when at last it came.

The first of the vexing questions to be settled was whether
Zionists would accept the Uganda proposal — or any other
proposal that offered a land other than Palestine for settlement. Zionists who supported Uganda were known as Territorialists — and their claims rocked the Seventh Congress,
which met (again in Basel) in 1905. After much bitter debate,
this Seventh Congress declared that Zionism could have no
other goal than Palestine itself. The Territorialists stalked
from the meeting — but their departure did not signal the collapse of the movement. Rather it signaled the emergence into
leadership of those (mostly from eastern Europe) who felt

that the movement must concentrate on the work of establishing more settlements in Palestine rather than pursuing the
will-o'-the-wisp of a charter. These men (known as "practicals" as opposed to "politicals") were inheritors of the old
Chovevei Zion spirit. Their instincts told them that the Zionist
Organization should attach itself more and more to the real
object of its desires, even if the prospects for full possession
seemed remote.

A bank had already been established — the Jewish Colonial
Trust — and, under the urging of the practicals, in 1908 the
World Zionist Organization established a colonizing agency in
Palestine itself. This was the Palestine Office, located in Jaffa
and directed with great energy by Arthur Ruppin. It organized, financed, and helped to establish many new settlements in the years following.

An event that stirred new and glowing hopes in the move-
ment was the Turkish revolution of 1908. On July 24 of that
year, a group of young Turkish army officers (known as the
Young Turks) forced Sultan Abdul-Hamid to grant a consti-
tutional regime to his decaying empire. In April, 1909, after
Abdul-Hamid attempted a counterrevolution, the Young
Turk forces occupied Constantinople and executed the sultan.
The Young Turks, headed by a "Committee of Union and
Progress," hoped to save their failing empire by cleansing the
government of inefficiency and corruption and introducing
Western political and industrial reforms.

At last, it seemed, that elusive charter might be in sight.
After all, two thirds of the population of the Ottoman Empire
was non-Turkish. There were Greeks, Serbs, Armenians,
Kurds, Arabs, Jews — and all had helped the insurgents overthrow the detested sultan. All wanted more autonomy within
the empire — and the Young Turk leaders listened sympa-
thetically to their demands. A branch of the Jewish Colonial

Trust was opened in Constantinople, and it seemed that the "politicals" might turn out to be right, after all.

But it was not long before the Young Turks revealed themselves as even more nationalistic than the sultan had been. They had extended the hand of friendship to their subject nationalities so long as they needed their help; once they were in power, that help was no longer necessary. The new Turkish government adopted repressive policies. They were determined to hang onto every last square yard of their empire and, for the sake of efficiency, they centralized its administration even more. Nor did they, as the Zionists had hoped, turn to England for guidance; instead they turned to the fount of anti-Semitism, the German Empire. They even went so far as to invite a German field marshal, Kolmar von der Goltz, to reorganize and train their new army.

All of which seemed to finally bury all hope of a charter. At the Tenth Zionist Congress, held in 1911, the "practicals" achieved complete control. This tenth congress also saw the emergence of what would become a bitter debate between those who favored Hebrew as an official language and those who favored Yiddish. While the Hebraists insisted that the Jewish language must be the language of the Bible and the Mishnah, and that only Hebrew could become a common tongue to a people who spoke all languages, the Yiddishists pointed out that Yiddish was the language of the great majority of the Jewish masses living in Germany, Poland, and Russia. Furthermore, an impressive literature already existed in that tongue. It had produced many writers of stature, such as the poet and writer of tales, Isaac Leib Peretz, "Sholem Aleichem" (Shalom Rabinovich, the "Jewish Mark Twain"), Mendele Mocher Seforim, the satirical novelist, and many others. This was a debate that would not soon be settled. But it was very apparent that Zionism had quickened, both in Hebrew and in Yiddish, the cultural life of Jews everywhere.

One of the far-flung branches of the Zionist movement — and one which would soon exert a decisive influence — was that established in the United States. It was in 1896, the year that Herzl published his *Judenstaat,* that a group of Russian immigrant Jews in Chicago organized themselves into what they optimistically called the "Chicago Zionist Organization Number One." The moving spirits of this group were the brothers Harris and Bernard Horvitch, both of whom had recently visited Palestine. They sent the journalist Leon Zolotkoff to Basel to represent them at the First Zionist Congress.

Of course, in America — itself a promised land to so many Jews — opposition to Zionism was intense. It brought into question basic loyalties and was seen as a bar to assimilation. To win more converts to their cause, the Chicagoans decided to copy certain other organizations. The Catholics had their Knights of Columbus; certain groups of workingmen had their Knights of Labor — and both were successful. So the Chicago Zionists reorganized themselves into the Knights of Zion, a fraternal order complete with secret signs, special handshakes, passwords, and all the other paraphernalia so dear to American hearts. The Knights of Zion prospered and by 1907 felt strong enough to drop their hocus-pocus. In that year they reconstituted themselves as the Federated Zionist Societies of the Middle West.

Although starting slightly later than their Chicago brethren, New York Jews, led by Richard Gottheil, a professor of Semitic languages at Columbia University, began organizing too. By July, 1898, representatives of more than one hundred different societies could meet in New York City to organize the Federation of American Zionists. In 1913 the Middle Western organization joined them. Prominent among the eastern leaders were such men as Morris Jastrow of Philadelphia, Scheftel

Schaffer of Baltimore, and Rabbi Stephen S. Wise of New
York.

The growth of the movement in America remained slow.
The rich held aloof from it for the same reasons that the
Rothschilds did in Europe. The federation was usually penniless; its official organ, *The Maccabean,* could be published
only once a month. First edited by Louis Lipsky, the monthly
later was managed by Jacob de Haas, a London journalist sent
expressly by Herzl to do the job. De Haas hung on as long as
he could — but financial problems finally forced him to leave
The Maccabean and move to Boston where he continued to
work for Zionism in the New World.

Zionism in America (as elsewhere) owed its vitality to the
poor Jews. Those few of the well-to-do who were willing to
lead them — the Wises, the Gottheils, the Jastrows, and others
— were like British officers in an army of "natives." So slow
and scattered was the growth of the movement in America that
it had but little strength to interest itself in such questions as
the Uganda proposal or the quarrel between "practicals" and
"politicals" which rocked the European movement. Yet progress was steady. American Zionists held conventions every year
and sent an increasing number of delegates to the World Congresses. In 1909 a youth movement called Young Judea was
created and, in 1912, the Women's Zionist Organization of
America was founded. It was called Hadassah (the Hebrew
name of the biblical Queen Esther) and among its founders
and leaders were Alice Seligsberg, Rose Jacobs, Irma Lind-
heim, and Eva Leon. But the commanding figure was Henri-
etta Szold, who by character and achievement showed herself to
be in the great tradition of Jewish women of history. The task
Hadassah assumed was to promote the health of Palestine by
combating its endemic diseases, such as trachoma and malaria,
and assisting its people (both Arabs and Jews) to better hy-

giene. This work (which has remained Hadassah's principal mission) was begun in 1913 with the dispatching of two trained nurses to establish a health center in Jerusalem. It was the modest start of what was to become a truly imposing network of hospitals, child-care centers, and other health institutions.

Meantime, under the auspices of the Palestine Office in Jaffa, the refugees of the bloody pogroms in which the Tsar drowned the Revolution of 1905 began arriving in the Holy Land. Known as the Second Aliyah, these Russian Jewish immigrants were fresh from the revolutionary ferment of their native land. Many had borne arms against the Tsar's Cossacks and many more were imbued with socialist ideals. They insisted that farming must be a cooperative venture — not one in which hired labor was exploited. Hence they organized collective farm settlements called *kevutzot*. They also insisted on the principle of Jewish self-defense.

What the second wave found when it arrived in Palestine was later recalled by one of its members, David Ben-Gurion. He arrived in 1906 and worked in various settlements during the next few years. "But," he reported, "I was down with malaria and I starved even more than I worked. My malaria was reliable and punctual, it visited me for four or five days every fortnight. I knew just when to expect it, and it never failed me. Hunger also was a faithful visitor. By day it was not too annoying, but at night it sometimes got out of hand and kept me from falling asleep."

In 1907, while working at the grain growing settlement of Ilaniyya in Lower Galilee, Ben-Gurion and his friend Isaac ben Zvi founded an organization of armed Jews to protect local settlements against marauders and brigands. Known as *Hashomer* (from the Hebrew for "watchman"), the defense force was an elite unit — applicants were accepted only after they had passed strict tests. Within a very short time its members became famous for hard riding and straight shooting. By 1914 nearly every Jewish settlement in Palestine was protected by Hashomer — and hostile Arabs suddenly had a new perception of Jews in general.

In December, 1909, Hashomer took part in the establishment of the first kevutzah at Deganyah in the upper Jordan Valley. It became known as the "mother of the kibbutzim," the model upon which, during the Third Aliyah, the kibbutzim were based. In a kibbutz everything was done by its own members, and the management was in the hands of committees elected to supervise different areas of activity. The members of the kibbutz received no wages, but all their needs — housing, food, clothing, and so on — were supplied by the kibbutz. Women had equal rights — and equal obligations — with the men, and special quarters, under expert charge, were provided for children. The kibbutzim did not, of course, spring full-blown from the minds of social philosophers or the exiled revolutionaries of 1905; they developed out of hard necessity and bitter experience. As new problems arose, new adjustments were made. Nor were the kibbutzim ideal societies in miniature; they lacked capital for the purchase of heavy machinery and land reclamation; they lacked, for a long time, the reserve population from which to recruit new members — and they had always to grapple with the problems of private personal property and an ever-growing demand for higher living standards. In short, they were as beset by human problems as any other type of social organization. But in the long run their worth was proven — for kibbutzim continue to thrive to this day.

The advance of the Jewish settlements in Palestine before the First World War would have been impossible without the Zionist movement and its organizations in Palestine; the

Anglo-Palestine Bank (a branch of the Jewish Colonial Trust); the Jewish National Fund, which began purchasing land in Palestine in 1905; and, of course, the Palestine Office in Jaffa, under the direction of the indefatigable Arthur Ruppin. Not all these organizations put together could muster the financial resources of a Rothschild — for example, the Jewish National Fund rarely received more than $50,000 in any year. But the Zionist organizations in Palestine possessed one asset which even the richest of Jewish philanthropists lacked — a goal, the great goal of restoring the Jewish people to nationhood. And behind this goal was the immeasurable sense of mission provided by the knowledge that millions of Jews all over the world had invested not only their pennies but their minds and hearts in Palestine.

Nor did the Jewish National Fund limit itself to purchasing land for agricultural settlements only. In 1909 it made a loan of $60,000 to sixty residents of the dirty, crowded Arab city of Jaffa — Jewish doctors, teachers, merchants, and others — with which to build a Jewish suburb north of the city. That loan meant the beginning of the city of Tel Aviv — the foundation stone for which was laid in a sea of yellow sand in 1909 by a small but stubborn group of idealists who would not heed the warnings of "practical" people. By 1914 Tel Aviv had a population of two thousand.

In 1904 there were some 60,000 Jews in Palestine; by 1914 the number had risen to 85,000. But of these, only 30,000 were Zionist immigrants; the rest continued to live on the philanthropy of Rothschilds and others, or the annual charity donations of Jewish synagogues around the world. For education, the entire Jewish population of Palestine was dependent upon private charity. Nearly all Jewish children were educated in schools set up and administered by French, German, or other foreign organizations — and were taught the languages of the schools. It was soon clear to Zionists all over the world — and especially to those in Palestine — that only by adopting Hebrew as the common everyday language of all Jews in Palestine could chaos be avoided. The resurrection of the language of the Bible demanded the modernization of that ancient tongue — a task undertaken by Eliezer ben Yehudah and other scholars, who adapted old words or invented new ones to describe things of which their ancestors had no knowledge.

As time passed, it became apparent that German and French school administrators were determined to impose their respective languages on students. Orthodox Jews also opposed the teaching of Hebrew, declaring that the holy language would only be profaned in daily use. A battle royal developed and went on for many years, with most teachers and students favoring Hebrew, while most school administrators and foreign philanthropists demanded that their own languages be taught. Yet the building of schools continued. At its Eleventh Congress in 1913, the Zionist Organization voted to build a university in Palestine and in that same year, under private auspices, the Haifa Technical Institute was organized. A handsome new building for it, on Mount Carmel, was opened during Passover week of 1914. Immediately the institute became embroiled in the language battle. Finally a compromise was reached whereby some classes would be taught in German (the language of the chief philanthropists behind the project) and some in Hebrew. But suddenly the language war in Palestine was overshadowed and engulfed by a greater struggle.

In August, 1914, the delicate, rickety, interlocked structures of European peace collapsed in the thunder of guns. The great powers — Germany and Austria-Hungary on one side, England, France, and Russia on the other — sent millions of men into battle. Soon the lesser nations of the Continent were drawn in, then other nations beyond the seas, and the great, prolonged agony of the "First" World War commenced. Out of all the death and destruction men everywhere hoped that a better world might emerge. But meanwhile, the Jews of Europe as well as those of Palestine were in deadly peril.

Everywhere in the warring nations Jews, like their fellow citizens, sprang to arms. Many hundreds of thousands fought in the armies of England, France, Germany, Austria — there were more than 700,000 Jews enlisted in the Tsarist Russian army alone. Yet this did not protect them from the nationalistic wrath of Russian and German patriots. When Russian generals suffered defeat (as they almost always did) against the Germans, their troubles were blamed on Russian Jews, who were said to be spying for the enemy. In areas conquered by the Germans, anti-Semitism was given a new impetus. Hundreds of thousands of Russian and Polish Jews — men, women and children — were packed into boxcars to remove them from the zones of operations — and sent to Siberia. Many perished on the way, more upon arrival in that desolate region. And wherever Russian armies did advance, as into Austria-Hungary, Jews perished by the thousands at the hands of the savage Cossacks.

In Palestine, the effects of war were equally disastrous. The exports of the Jewish settlements — mostly oranges, wine, and almonds — were cut off by blockades and counterblockades established by the warring powers. Worse than that was the entry of the Ottoman Empire into the war on the side of Germany. This meant that Jews of Russian, English, or French nationality were automatically enemy aliens in Palestine. Furthermore, the Turkish government declared that Zionism was a plot to dismember their empire. Jemal Pasha, the Turkish commander in Syria and Palestine, accused the Jews of planning to set up their own government. He dissolved the Hashomer defense forces and confiscated their guns, closed the Anglo-Palestine Bank, and exiled or arrested many Jewish leaders. As the war progressed and Turkish fears grew, many thousands of Jews were driven into exile in Egypt (then ruled by Great Britain) and Syria. Jemal's repressions were, at least, impartial; he also accused the Palestinian Arabs of plotting a rebellion. Many of them too were exiled, imprisoned, or executed.

Jemal Pasha was not entirely wrong in his suspicions. Palestinian Jews, seeing no future for themselves or Zionism under the corrupt and reactionary Turkish tyranny, welcomed a British invasion of the decadent Ottoman Empire. Some supplied information to the British (for which a few were hanged as spies by the Turks), while many more enlisted in the British army then gathering in Egypt. And the Arabs were indeed planning a rebellion — for they too had endured too much too long from their hated Turkish overlords. Led by the fabulous Englishman T. E. Lawrence ("Lawrence of Arabia") the desert tribes soon embarked on a widespread guerrilla war of liberation against the Turks and their German "advisors."

Meanwhile the World Zionist Organization was in desperate straits. Its two strongest communities, the Russian and the German, now stood on opposite sides of the battle lines in Europe. War disrupted its international activities and forced the relocation of its headquarters to neutral Copenhagen in Denmark. From there the European Zionist leadership could do almost nothing to help the settlements in Palestine — and less to help the Jews of Russia and Poland. At a time when so many Jews faced such dire peril, it seemed that Zionism would be impotent to protect them. Only from neutral America, with its relatively weak and disorganized Zionist community, could any help at all be expected. And in this hour of crisis a new American leader emerged.

He was one of America's great native sons — Louis D. Brandeis, a Boston lawyer, whose friendship with Jacob de Haas (the former editor of *The Maccabean*) had sparked a first interest in the Zionist dream. Brandeis was born in 1856 in Louisville, Kentucky, the son of Czech refugees from the lost Revolution of 1848. He attended law school at Harvard, practiced law for a while in St. Louis, and then set up practice in Boston. His law practice was an immediate success — but his interests went far beyond that. He became known as the "people's lawyer," a champion of the common man against the giant corporations, the industrial monopolies, and what he called the "curse of bigness." He represented the public interest against utilities, insurance companies, and unfair employers. He became a symbol of liberal thought and purpose in America and, when in 1916 President Woodrow Wilson appointed him an associate justice of the United States Supreme Court, the groan that emerged from Wall Street was, one reporter declared, "like the echo of a great national disaster."

Brandeis, it seems, was fully converted to the Zionist cause in 1912, through the influence of Jacob de Haas. He was intrigued by the Zionist dream and deeply impressed by the work of Theodor Herzl. Furthermore, it seemed to Brandeis that Zionism was in harmony with his highest ideals: the liberation of men from oppression and the extension of the boundaries of freedom. Everything Brandeis thought of as true Americanism he found in Zionism. "To be good Americans," he said, "we must be better Jews, and to be better Jews we must become Zionists." In the years preceeding the First World War, Brandeis's voice had a special impact upon educated American Jews. Yet the American Zionist movement remained feeble. Of the three million Jews then living in the United States no more than fifty or sixty thousand belonged to any of the Zionist organizations.

Then came the outbreak of war in Europe in August, 1914.
On August 30 "an extraordinary conference of representatives
of American Zionism" met in New York. The call to the conference, issued by Louis Lipsky, declared: "The Organization
in Europe is shattered. . . . It is our first and most holy duty to
hold and maintain in this critical moment the Zionist Organization, and especially the positions we have won . . . in
Palestine." The conference established a "provisional executive committee," to represent all the American Zionist organizations, issued a call for an emergency fund of $200,000 for the
immediate needs of the Palestinian settlements, and, most importantly of all, elected Louis D. Brandeis chairman of the
executive committee. Brandeis threw himself into the task
with typical energy and consummate ability. His chairmanship
also enlisted the support of various individuals of great distinction, such as Felix Frankfurter, Bernard Flexner, Benjamin Victor Cohen, and Nathan Straus. "Organize, organize,
organize," said Brandeis, "until every Jew in America must
stand up and be counted."

In November, 1914, the various Jewish organizations which
had assumed the burden of relief for the settlements in Palestine were organized into the American Jewish Joint Distribution Committee (JDC). By 1916 more than $6,000,000 had
been raised by the JDC — not only for the Jews of Palestine,
but also for the Jews of eastern Europe. In 1917 $10,000,000
was gathered. In March, 1915, the American collier *Vulcan*
left Philadelphia for Jaffa with nearly a thousand tons of food
for distribution in Palestine — not only to Jews, but also to
Moslems and Christians in the Holy Land. But this was not the
first aid to reach Jaffa. The first aid was $50,000 that Henry
Morgenthau, the United States ambassador to Turkey, had
gathered and sent on to Arthur Ruppin at the Palestine Office.
What made this modest gift of money important was that it

arrived in Jaffa aboard an American warship — a foreshadow-
ing of things to come.

While Brandeis labored to strengthen the Zionist movement
in America, significant events were unfolding in London.
There the Zionist forces were led by Dr. Chaim Weizmann —
the chemist who had explained his people's attachment to
Jerusalem to Prime Minister Balfour only a few years before.
Weizmann, long a prominent figure at Zionist congresses, was
born in a hamlet near the city of Pinsk in Polish Russia in
1874. He had studied at the Universities of Berlin and Geneva,
and from 1904 to 1916 had been teaching chemistry at the
University of Manchester. He had long been considered a
"practical" among Zionists — one who had little confidence
in the pursuit of "charters" or other total solutions. He had
favored the real work of settlement in Palestine and was particularly immersed in the struggle to establish a university
there. But now, suddenly, in a world gone mad, a great opportunity was presented.

It was clear that no matter which side won the war, the
Ottoman Empire would not survive. If the Germans won they
would reduce the Turkish dominions to vassal states; if the
Allies won they would dismember the sultan's domains. Already, the English and French were secretly negotiating to set
up puppet Arab states in the Near East and establish colonies
there in the event of their victory. But that victory was by no
means assured. The titanic struggle taking place in Europe was
too evenly balanced for the Allies to ignore any possible help.
The support of world Jewry might just make the difference
between victory and defeat — especially the support of American Jews, who might be able to influence Woodrow Wilson to
enter the war on the Allied side. What, in all this, would be
the fate of Palestine?

Early in the war Weizmann had devised a new process for

the large-scale production of acetone, a substance essential in the manufacture of explosives. This success won him an opportunity to speak. Lloyd George, at that time chairman of the British War Munitions Committee, asked Weizmann what recognition he desired for his brilliant work. Weizmann replied: "I would like you to do something for my people," and went on to plead the Zionist cause. Two years later Lloyd George would become prime minister — and remember Weizmann's words.

Meantime Weizmann began to build up a group of influential Jews and non-Jews to gain support for Zionism in official government circles. He was joined in this task by Nahum Sokolow, who had been dispatched by the Copenhagen committee to enlist Allied support. Among those who followed Weizmann were Viscount Samuel, who was to become British Home Secretary in 1916, Lionel Walter, Lord Rothschild, Charles P. Scott, editor of the influential *Manchester Guardian*, and Henry Wickham Steed, editor of *The Times* of London. All these men, and many others, were determined that in the new world order that would emerge from the shambles of war, the goals of the Jewish people should be recognized.

Still there were obstacles. Britain would not act without the support of her allies, France and Russia. But the Tsar and his ministers remained bitter foes of Zionism — and the French feared to offend them. Furthermore, a Jewish Palestine might upset British and French colonial ambitions in the Near East. And then, in generating Arab rebellion against the Turks, certain British officers had made all sorts of promises to Arab leaders — promises which in some cases ran directly counter to Zionist aspirations.

In the spring of 1917, however, came important changes.

First, Russia was swept by revolution and, for all intents and purposes, left the war. The Tsar's prejudices no longer needed to be consulted. Second, in April, 1917, the United States entered the war — and Wilson's was a powerful voice in support of Zionism. Then too there had been a change in the British government; Lloyd George was now Prime Minister, Sir Herbert Samuel became Secretary of State for Home Affairs, and Arthur James Balfour became Secretary of State for Foreign Affairs. All three were ardent friends of Zionism. Finally, there was the undeniable fact that in the spring of 1917 the war was not going well. Russia and her vast manpower had retired from the field; American manpower was not yet engaged; Italy had suffered disastrous defeats at the hands of the Germans and Austrians; the French army was on the verge of mutiny — and the Germans were concentrating for yet another massive blow against the Western Front. In such circumstances the Allies were willing to pay almost any price for support from any quarter, even the Zionists. Years later, Lloyd George was to recall: "The Zionist leaders gave us a definite promise that, if the Allies committed themselves to give facilities for the establishment of a national home for the Jews in Palestine, they would do their best to rally Jewish sentiment and support throughout the world to the Allied cause. They have kept their word."

Negotiations were delicate and prolonged, but through the tireless efforts of Weizmann in London, Sokolow in Paris, and Brandeis in Washington, they finally bore fruit. In the fall of 1917 Baron Rothschild received a letter from the British Foreign Office. It was dated November 2 and signed by Arthur James Balfour, His Majesty's Secretary for Foreign Affairs. It read:

"I have much pleasure in conveying to you, on behalf of His

Majesty's Government, the following declaration of sympathy
with Jewish Zionist aspirations which has been submitted to,
and approved by, the Cabinet:

" 'His Majesty's Government view with favour the establishment in Palestine of a national home for the Jewish people,
and will use their best endeavours to facilitate the achievement of this object, it being clearly understood that nothing
shall be done which may prejudice the civil and religious
rights of existing non-Jewish communities in Palestine, or the
rights and political status enjoyed by Jews in any other country.'

"I should be grateful if you would bring this declaration to
the knowledge of the Zionist Federation."

At the end of his long and brilliantly successful life, Arthur
Balfour was reported to have said of the declaration which
bore his name that "on the whole [it] had been the thing
'he' looked back upon as the most worth 'his' doing."

The Balfour Declaration was not quite the "charter" of
which Herzl had dreamed. In keeping with British diplomatic
tradition, its wording was fuzzy and liable to many interpretations. But as they all later stated, there was never any question
in the minds of those who made this promise that what was
meant was the creation of a Jewish state in Palestine. And so
the Jews understood it. All over the world enthusiastic celebrations took place. In revolutionary Odessa more than
100,000 people cheered in the streets; in New York, London,
Paris, Washington, Chicago, Petrograd, and hundreds of lesser
towns Jewish communities gave thanks. Religious leaders of
every faith hailed the Declaration as the fulfillment of ancient
biblical prophesy. A new Jewish Commonwealth would now
be created — and the world would be young again.

But Palestine was still a part of the Ottoman Empire, controlled by powerful Turkish and German military forces.

Hard fighting lay ahead, and Jews everywhere realized that only he who fights for victory may claim a share in its spoils. Thus was born the Jewish Legion. It was recruited from among those Palestinian Jews who had been driven into Egypt by the Turks, and also included many English, American, French, and Canadian volunteers — men who, for one reason or another, had been denied a place in the Allied armies (in which more than one and a half million Jews served during the war) but who now saw a chance to fight for a new homeland.

Comprising first one battalion, later several battalions, of His Majesty's Royal Fusiliers, the Jewish Legion (they wore the Shield of David shoulder patch) formed part of the Egyptian Expeditionary Force, commanded by General Sir Edmund Allenby, which invaded Palestine early in 1917. After a brilliant campaign, on December 9, 1917, Allenby's forces entered Jerusalem. The fall of the Holy City, after so many centuries of Moslem rule, made a tremendous impression on the entire world. But this was far from the end of Allenby's campaign to liberate Palestine. In September, 1918, the second phase began. And the Jewish Legion was a part of that valiant force that cut a path through the Turkish and German lines and then held open the "gate" through which Allenby poured his fifty thousand Australian cavalrymen in a charge that destroyed the Turkish army and dealt the death blow to the Ottoman Empire. For the first time in nearly two thousand years — since the Romans vanquished Bar Kochba — Jewish military formations had fought and won a victory in their ancient homeland.

Haggada:

The Fall of Jerusalem

". . . Early in the morning of the ninth, when the last Turk had departed, houses, caves, cellars and hovels discharged their occupants who rushed into the streets with excited shouts of triumph and relief. Mothers, sons, fathers and daughters, with all their kinfolk, fell on each other's necks, sobbing and laughing with joy at the deliverance. Exactly two thousand and eighty-two years ago to this day, in 165 B.C., when Judas Maccabeus recaptured the Temple from the Seleucids, similar scenes must have been enacted. . . .

"On December eleventh the commander-in-chief, accompanied by representatives of the Allies, made his formal entrance into Jerusalem. . . .

"The historic Jaffa Gate was opened, after years of disuse, for the purpose and he was thus enabled to pass into the Holy City. . . . When the time came for the great and simple act of the solemn entry of General Allenby into Jerusalem . . . the inhabitants mustered courage to gather in a great crowd. . . . Many wept for joy, priests were seen to embrace one another, but there were no theatricalities. . . . The General entered the city on foot and left it on foot, and throughout the ceremony no Allied flag was flown, while naturally no enemy flags were visible.

"A proclamation announcing that order would be maintained in all the hallowed sites of the three great religions, which were to be guarded and preserved for free use of worshippers, was read in English, French, Arabic, Hebrew, Greek, Russian and Italian, from the terrace of the entrance to the citadel below the Tower of David. When this was done, the chief notables and ecclesiastics of the different communities who had remained in Jerusalem were presented to General Allenby. After this brief ceremony the commander-in-chief left the city by the Jaffa Gate. . . .

"After General Allenby had entered Jerusalem modestly on foot, many of the Arab rulers recalled their cherished prophecy — He who shall save Jerusalem and exalt her among the nations will enter the city on foot, and his name will be 'God, the Prophet' — *Allah Nebi!*"

> — *from Major Raymond Savage's* Allenby of Armageddon

8

The Mandate

It is a wonderful country. . . . The age-long longing — the love is all explicable now. . . . The way is long, the path difficult, but the struggle is worthwhile. It is indeed a Holy Land.

LOUIS D. BRANDEIS

So Zionism — that utopian fantasy — was suddenly at the end of the First World War a very real factor in international politics and an integral part of Allied peace plans. But if the Jews seemed much closer to the goals of Zionism at the end of the war than when it began, the urgency of their achievement had become desperate — as desperate as the position of Eastern Jewry after 1918.

With the breakup of the Tsarist Empire, many of its subject peoples experienced a wave of fiery nationalism — especially the Poles and the Ukrainians. Pogroms were, of course, an old tradition in Poland and in the Ukraine — and as a new Polish nation came into being out of the wreckage of Tsarist imperialism, a wave of savage outbreaks against the Jews swept that unhappy land. The Jews in Lvov, Pinsk, Wilno, Lida, and a score of other cities suffered a new martyrdom. The worst disaster fell upon the Jews in the Ukraine — for there they were massacred by both sides in the civil war which ravaged that area. Tsarist counterrevolutionary armies, Bolshevik armies, independent marauding hordes — all campaigned in the Ukraine for years — and all committed outrages upon defenseless Jewish communities. Hundreds of thousands of Jews were murdered before the Communist regime finally won full control of the Russian nation in 1920. Then the pogroms, at least, came to an end. But they were replaced by the bitterly anti-Zionist policies of the new government. Zionism, in Russian Communist eyes, was no more than a reactionary, counter-revolutionary plot. If it was religious then it was "unscientific" and "regressive" in the new atheist society; if it was national, then it was an attempt to break up the Russian nation; if it was political it was a plot against the new dictatorship. Zionists were branded state criminals by the new society — and were persecuted with zeal. Russian Jewry, which before the war had been in the vanguard of Zionism, was now reduced to impotence.

In the new Poland, while pogroms and anti-Semitic outrages received official encouragement, Zionism was not proscribed, and Polish Jews, although reduced to pauperism, continued to play a leading role in the movement. Nearly forty percent of the immigrants who came to Palestine between the two World Wars were Polish Jews. But the Jews of Poland, like the Jews of the new Soviet Union, were in no position to contribute anything besides their flesh and spirit to Zionism — they could not help in the urgent task of raising the money needed to develop the new National Home.

That task might have been undertaken by American Jews — but they were badly divided. Despite the work of Brandeis, the Jewish Committee, and the Zionist Federation, most American Jews were still not enlisted under the Zionist banner — and those who were were divided into several groups. It was not until December, 1918, that a new organization was formed which embraced all the various Zionist committees: the American Jewish Congress. The congress, meeting in Philadelphia, approved the Balfour Declaration and urged that Great Britain be appointed to administer Palestine under the mandate of the soon-to-be-created League of Nations.

The mandate system, like the League of Nations itself, was one of the pet dreams of Woodrow Wilson and other progressive Allied statesmen. The idea was that instead of the victorious Allies simply grabbing off the former colonial possessions of the German and Ottoman empires — places like Syria, East Africa, Melanesia, Palestine — they would govern them under the authority of and as trustees for the League of Nations. Thus the newly "liberated" territories would not become mere colonies again; instead, the Mandatory Powers would "guide" the presumably "backward" native populations in economic development and toward eventual self-government and total independence. While idealists hailed this as a "responsible" solution, realists in London, Paris, and Washington recognized it immediately as a perfect cover for colonialism and continued exploitation.

Needless to say, American Jews, like their European brethren, were to be counted among the idealists. They welcomed the idea of a British mandate over Palestine — for they naturally assumed that such a mandate would be based on the Balfour Declaration, thereby giving legal substance to what was still only a promise. Under the umbrella of British administration the work of establishing a Jewish National Home could proceed peacefully and rapidly.

But this Zionist vision met several immediate obstacles. The first of these was financial. With the restoration of peace, the flow of money into Zionist coffers from the American, English, and French Jewish communities was reduced to a trickle. Charity is an impulse, not a sustained effort, among most people, and too many Western Jews simply assumed that the crisis

for which they had mobilized their resources was now finally
ended. Then, as the years passed, worldwide recessions merged
into the universal misery of the Great Depression and money
simply wasn't available.

The second obstacle to Zionist hopes was, predictably, the
hostility of the Arabs. With their liberation from the Turks,
nationalism spread through the Arab world. New Arab states
— Syria, Iraq, Lebanon, and Transjordan — came into being
under British or French "protection," and their rulers jock-
eyed for political position and territory. All viewed Palestine
as a legitimate prize of war — and none would tolerate the
establishment there of a Jewish state or, for that matter, continued Jewish immigration into the Holy Land.

The third and greatest barrier to Zionist work in Palestine
was, oddly enough, the opposition of Great Britain — the
power which had sponsored the Jewish National Home in the
first place. British opposition should not have surprised anyone. For more than a century England had been dependent,
economically, politically, and militarily, upon its vast empire
— an empire maintained by sea power and the cunning of a
handful of politicians ruling hundreds of millions of people.
Among those hundreds of millions, very many were Moslem —
and English politicians felt that they dared not risk affronting
the Arabs of the Near East for fear that they might touch off a
rebellion that would undermine British influence from Cairo
to Singapore. Furthermore, the "jewel" of the British Empire
was India — and the sea lifeline to that subcontinent ran
through the Suez Canal. It was for this reason that the British
had established a "protectorate" over Egypt, and for this reason that they sought domination of the new Near Eastern nations. Fear of a widespread Arab uprising and anxiety over
their Suez sea route to the east always underlay British policy
in Palestine — that and a kind of snobbish anti-Semitism which

cropped up frequently among English military men and upper-class Foreign Office officials.

No sooner had the Turkish army been defeated than various Arab leaders began plotting to create empires of their own. The Emir Feisal dreamed of a "Greater Syria," which should embrace Syria, Iraq, Transjordan, and Palestine; the Emir Abdullah in Transjordan dreamed of establishing a Jordanian state that would include Jordan, Palestine, and Lebanon; Amin El Husseini, soon to be appointed leader of the Near Eastern Moslem religious community, with the title Grand Mufti of Jerusalem, dreamed of nothing less than a new Jihad (Holy War), which would establish a new Arabian Empire from Baghdad to the Straits of Gibraltar. None of the Arab leaders was prepared to accept French or British domination — and none was prepared to accept a Jewish National Home. The diversion of Arab hostility from themselves to the Jews — the eternal scapegoat — became one of the weapons in the British and French imperialist arsenal which helped them keep the Arabs in subjection.

The partition of the late, unlamented Ottoman Empire was to take place at a meeting of the victorious Allies in San Remo in 1920. There the claims of both Arabs and Jews would receive "consideration," while Britain and France carved out their new "spheres of influence" in the Near East. Hoping to convince the Allied statesmen that they would never accept a Jewish homeland in their midst, Palestinian Arabs, urged on (and armed) by Emir Feisal, began widespread rioting against the Jewish community. Large bands of well-armed Bedouins (Arab desert nomads) attacked the Jewish settlements of Kfar Giladi and Tel Hai in northern Palestine. Led by Joseph Trumpeldor, the colonists at Tel Hai resisted Arab onslaughts for several months. Then, on March 1, 1920, under a flag of truce, a number of Arabs were permitted to enter the stronghold. The Arabs, once inside, opened fire, killing Trumpeldor and several of his companions. Tel Hai had to be abandoned — but was shortly afterward reconquered. Trumpeldor's last words were "Never mind, it is good to die for our country."

On April 2, 1920, many thousands of Arabs rioted in Jerusalem, and more lives were lost — both Jewish and Arab. What, it may be asked, were the British Occupation Forces doing all this time? Why did they not intervene? Time and again they were warned by various Jewish leaders of impending Arab violence. They did intervene; when the rioting broke out in Jerusalem, the British police and army prevented Jewish self-defense groups from reaching that city. They arrested several Jewish leaders and imprisoned them. The British military leaders in Palestine (Allenby had long since gone home) were so infected with anti-Semitism that many of them secretly hoped for an Arab victory, and in the end their benign indifference encouraged the Arabs to even further violence.

But the violence boomeranged. No government can yield to rioters, nor can it permit subordinate military officials to dictate official policy. So on April 24, 1920, the Supreme Council of the Allied Powers, meeting in San Remo, voted to declare Palestine a British Mandated Territory — the mandate to be administered in accordance with the aims of the Balfour Declaration. This decision was made part of the peace treaty with Turkey — the Treaty of Sèvres. Thus the good intentions of the Balfour Declaration became the juridical reality of the mandate, and the Jewish National Home became an official part of the new world order. Furthermore, Britain appointed Sir Herbert Samuel, the ardently Zionist former Home Secretary, to head up its administration in Palestine. He arrived at Jaffa on July 1, 1920. Surely now, at last, peaceful progress could begin.

But what of the Arab leaders and their dreams? The new

British High Commissioner, in an attempt to mollify Pales-
tinian Arabs, confirmed Amin El Husseini as Grand Mufti of
Jerusalem. This was to prove a disastrous error. Then, in 1921,
the French, consolidating their hold over Syria, drove King
Feisal from his throne. Thereupon Feisal's brother Abdullah
gathered an army in Transjordan and vowed to drive the
French into the sea. Matters were finally settled when King
Feisal was made ruler of Iraq and his brother Abdullah the
Emir of Transjordan — with a large British subsidy. At one
stroke this settlement cut the huge and sparsely populated region east of the River Jordan from Palestine — of which it had
always, historically, been a part. The turmoil reached into
Palestine (with the encouragement of the Grand Mufti) and,
on May 1, 1921, Arab mobs rioted against Jews in Jaffa and
Tel Aviv. The violence was stemmed by the arrival of Jewish
self-defense units, but casualties were heavy on both sides.

In the summer of 1922, the British government issued an
official White Paper on Palestine. It was calculated to appease
Arab anger. It formalized the removal of the Transjordan
area from the sphere of Jewish colonization, denied that the
Balfour Declaration had meant the creation of a Jewish state
in Palestine, and announced a policy of strict control over
Jewish immigration, which would be limited to the "economic
absorptive capacity" of the country. It did allow that a Jewish
"National Home" (not a "state") would be fostered in Palestine. Zionist leaders in London were required to sign their acceptance of these "explanations" or face even harsher British
policies. They signed. But the Arabs did not. They demanded
the total revocation of the Balfour Declaration and a complete
halt to all Jewish immigration into Palestine. British appeasement of the Arabs did not work then or at any later time. Nonetheless, on July 24, 1922, the council of the newly formed
League of Nations, meeting in Geneva, finally ratified the

Palestine Mandate in all its particulars. It would seem that if documents, declarations, treaties, and Official Papers could establish a Jewish National Home, then the project ought to succeed. With the League of Nations Mandate, it appeared that at long last Herzl's "Charter" was a reality.

Meanwhile, the Zionist movement was suffering from factionalism. A conference of Zionist leaders from all over the world had met in London in the spring of 1920. It was supposed to assess the damage done to the movement by the war, try to knit together the now-shattered World Congress Organization, and lay plans for new and enlarged activity in Palestine. The American delegation was headed by Louis Brandeis, the English by Chaim Weizmann. But from the beginning it was apparent that these two great leaders could not agree. Brandeis felt that official acceptance of the mandate as expressed in the various declarations and treaties had fulfilled the political aims of Zionism. From now on Zionists should turn from politics, propaganda, and education to the more practical work of economic enterprise in Palestine. Furthermore, this enterprise and its financing should be under expert control. Non-Zionists as well as Zionists should be encouraged to invest in the new projects. Charity was well and good — but investment was, in the long run, more fruitful.

Weizmann, while agreeing that practical work in Palestine must by all means proceed, was not at all convinced that the political task of Zionism was now ended, that its propaganda and education work should cease. Moreover, he distrusted the idea that non-Zionists should be encouraged to invest in Zionist projects. For investment means control — and control of economic enterprise has a way of extending itself into other forms of social and political control. Matters came to a climax when the European delegates, headed by Weizmann, voted to establish a fund of some twenty-five million pounds for Pales-

tinian settlement for a five-year plan of development. This
fund was to include both investments and gifts and would
finance the entire National Home program. Brandeis refused
to support this "mingling of funds" proposal and, before the
conference ended, Brandeis and the other Americans walked
out.

In June, 1921, American Zionists met in convention in
Cleveland. There the actions of the American delegation to
the London conference came under sharp attack. The American withdrawal was seen as a blow to the entire world movement. Weizmann and several of his supporters had toured
America that spring, urging Zionists throughout the country
to support the new Foundation Fund. Although his reception
from Brandeis, Mack and other leaders was cool, he was received everywhere by the Jewish masses as the statesman and
the architect of the Jewish National Home — a savior. Weizmann's support in Cleveland proved overwhelming. The convention voted to support the Foundation Fund. The views of
Julian Mack (president of the Zionist Organization of America), Felix Frankfurter, Stephen Wise, and other apostles of
Brandeis were defeated. Under the circumstances, these and
other prominent leaders had no choice but to resign from
their positions in the Zionist Organization of America — as did
Louis Brandeis himself. American Zionists would henceforth
give all-out support to the World Zionist Organization under
Weizmann's leadership.

It was under the cloud of this rupture within the American
movement that the Twelfth Zionist Congress met in Prague in
September, 1921. The debate, centering on the American
split, was stormy and prolonged, but in the end the congress
adopted the Foundation Fund and elected Weizmann president of the World Zionist Organization. There were reasons
for confidence as well as anxiety. From September, 1920, to

April, 1921, some ten thousand new immigrants had entered
Palestine. These were but the vanguard of the Third Aliyah —
a new "wave" of immigration, which was heartening because
so many of its members were youthful pioneers, men and
women who were determined to drain swamps, build roads,
and undertake all the arduous tasks of creating a new environment in the Holy Land. Furthermore, an elected assembly
representing all the Jews of Palestine had met in October,
1920. Called the *Asephat ha-Nivcharim* (Representative Assembly), it had chosen a National Council (*Vaad Leumi*),
which was recognized by the British as the governing body of
Palestinian Jewry. And, finally, the Twelfth Congress itself
was cause for rejoicing — for the delegates now represented
nearly a million dues-paying members in almost all civilized
countries. The congress denounced Arab violence — but also
proclaimed "our determination to live with the Arab people
on terms of concord and mutual respect." As for Brandeis and
the dissident Americans — it was hoped and predicted that
before very long they would return to the fold.

Meanwhile hard times had come to Palestine. A postwar
depression in Europe and the United States brought about a
slump in the market for Palestinian exports, and the new
waves of immigrants were creating an unemployment problem. Many Jews were now leaving Palestine in search of better
opportunities elsewhere. In 1923 there were 7,420 arrivals —
but 3,465 departures. While Zionism could do nothing effec-
tive to bring the world out of depression it could certainly do
something about unemployment in Palestine. Unemployment
in a land where everything was yet to be built? All that was
required was capital to finance the hundreds and thousands of
projects, settlements, and dreams of the Palestinians. Money
was the problem.

As had almost always been the case, rich Jews were, by and

large, non-Zionists. Generally they maintained a low political
profile and, as Jews, preferred to be thought of as totally assimilated. While they might be persuaded to support cultural
or charitable activities in the Holy Land, they would not give
money to support the controversial political aim of the
Zionists — the creation of a Jewish state. The Foundation
Fund, administered through the Jewish Agency, continued to
lack money. Weizmann and Sokolow had come to believe that
only by encouraging non-Zionist Jewish participation in the
agency could sufficient funds be acquired. Most members of
the Zionist Congress understood this — but they distrusted
participation in the agency by those who were opposed to the
eventual aim of creating a Jewish state. This issue — of enlarg-
ing the Agency and permitting non-Zionists to participate in
its decisions — continued to agitate the movement and its congresses for the next several years. And even though Weizmann
continued to win support for his policy (by small majorities)
he did not find it easy to enlist non-Zionist Jews under Jewish
Agency leadership. For example, in 1924 Weizmann attended
a conference of non-Zionists in New York. Many noble words
were spoken about the duty of Jews everywhere, whether or
not they were Zionists, to help rebuild Palestine for the honor
of the Jewish name — but funds were voted not for the Jewish
Agency but rather for the Palestine Economic Corporation,
which had been founded some time before and which acted
independently of Jewish Agency control. In that same year,
non-Zionist American Jews contributed fifteen million dollars
toward the settlement of Jews in agricultural communities,
not in Palestine, but in the Ukraine. There was no need to
question the sincerity of the Soviet government in allocating
lands for this purpose. Their aim, after all, was the total assimilation of all people under Communist rule and the extin-

guishing of all national, religious, or even cultural sentiments which might threaten their totalitarian regime. Communist leaders in Russia understood perfectly well that resettlement of Russian Jews within the Soviet empire struck a blow at Zionist dreams.

In that same year of 1924, economic conditions in Palestine began to improve. A new wave of Jewish immigrants was now entering the land — the Fourth Aliyah. Since United States immigration quota laws of 1921 and 1924 had had the effect of reducing the admittance of Jews to one tenth of the prewar level, increasing numbers were forced to turn to Palestine. In 1924 nearly thirteen thousand arrived; in 1925 more than thirty-four thousand. This Fourth Aliyah was composed, for the most part, of middle-class businessmen and professionals. Most came from Poland, where an official anti-Semitism was trying to legislate them out of existence; some came from Russia, refugees from Communist anti-Zionism. They brought with them capital and skills which had been wanting among previous waves of immigration — and recovery from the post-war economic slump was rapid. In a moving affirmation of faith in the future, on April 1, 1925, on Mount Scopus, opposite Jerusalem, the Hebrew University was inaugurated. An audience of seven thousand listened to addresses by Weizmann, Herbert Samuel — and Lord Arthur Balfour. The seventy-year-old British statesman who had done so much to help the Zionist cause invoked the great tradition of Jewish scholarship and predicted an even greater future. With only a library and three study units, the university, like the National Home itself, was but an infant — but its birth was the occasion of celebrations among Jewish communities throughout the world.

With the economic situation in Palestine improving, the

Fourteenth World Zionist Congress, which met in Vienna in August, 1925, opened on a note of hope. But it met also in an atmosphere of renewed urgency.

This was only the second World Zionist Congress to have met in Vienna, the city of Theodor Herzl, but in the years since 1913, the old anti-Semitism of the Austrian capital had become grimmer, more ferocious. Across the border in Germany an Austrian-born politician named Adolf Hitler was preaching to larger and larger audiences his insane hatred of the Jews — a hatred more virulent, obscene, and frightful than anything ever heard before. Although not yet a major power in German politics, Hitler had already published his book, *Mein Kampf (My Battle)*, in which he frankly and openly proclaimed his aims of world conquest — and the utter extermination of the Jewish people. *Mein Kampf* was becoming the Bible of anti-Semites everywhere and, in Vienna, howling mobs led by swastika-bearing Nazis (members of Hitler's National Socialist Party) attacked the building in which the Zionist Congress met. Only the intervention of heavily armed police cordons saved the delegates from lynching. Nonetheless, the congress proceeded with its work. Again it authorized Weizmann to enlist non-Zionists in the Jewish Agency — this time with certain safeguards against their deflecting the agency from its Zionist goals.

It would eventually turn out that all this debate over admitting non-Zionists into the agency was a waste of breath. When, four years later (in 1929 at Zurich) the enlarged Jewish Agency finally came into being, prominent non-Zionist Jewish leaders from several countries joined the agency in one capacity or another. But within a very short time the agency reverted to a totally Zionist organization. For the non-Zionists soon lost interest in its work and, one by one, retired from active membership. Zionism, it appeared, was too radical, too positive, too unique, too committed a movement to long enlist the energies of those whose entire hearts, minds, and souls were not dedicated to its aims.

During the years after 1925 the fortunes of the Jews in Palestine fluctuated between prosperity and depression, peace with the Arabs and renewed strife. From 1925 to 1928, while Field Marshal Lord Plumer was British High Commissioner, peace reigned. This was largely due to the fact that Lord Plumer was a soldier who would stand for no threats from the Arabs. He also proved to be a liberal statesman. He improved the lot of Arab tenant farmers, set up regulations to protect industrial workers, introduced a Palestinian currency (which replaced the Egyptian money in use until then) and, to relieve unemployment, instituted a program of public works, including road building and the drainage of marshes.

By 1929 the Jews of Palestine already constituted a national entity — a state in miniature. Even though immigration was strictly controlled by the British, the Jewish population of the Holy Land had risen to 162,000. Where, in 1914, there had been fewer than 50 Jewish settlements in the countryside, there were now 120. The population of Tel Aviv, 2,000 in 1914, was over 40,000 in 1929, and new Jewish suburbs were rising near Haifa and the Old City of Jerusalem. There was an electric company, there were cement works, oil refineries, flour mills, and other industrial enterprises — and there were trade unions. The General Federation of Hebrew Workers in Israel (*Histadrut* for short), founded in 1920, was already busily establishing various cooperative enterprises and, in 1929 founded its own political party, *Mapai* (the word consists of the Hebrew initials of *Miphliget Poale Eretz Israel*, "Party of the Workers of the Land of Israel"). There were now more than 220 schools with more than 20,000 pupils, and the Hadassah Medical Organization had established a network of hos-

pitals and health centers. The overall governing body of Palestinian Jews, the *Knesset Israel,* through its Representative
Assembly and its National Council, enjoyed the power to tax
its constituents and, under supervision of the British authorities, to regulate their affairs.

If all this progress was apparent to Jews, it was also apparent
to the Arab leaders. Those leaders, especially the Grand Mufti
of Jerusalem, depended for their support upon the hard-
earned coins of the poor Arab masses of Palestine. But more
and more Arabs were benefiting from Jewish enterprise. More
and more of them were awakening to the modern world from
the slumber in which their own leaders wished them to remain. The growth of a Jewish Commonwealth in Palestine
threatened to lift the Arab masses there, and elsewhere, into
an awareness of just how ruthlessly their leaders were exploiting them. Something had to be done — and the Grand Mufti
decided to inflame religious passions.

In August, 1929, agents of the Grand Mufti began spreading
rumors among Palestinian Arabs that the Jews planned to attack and seize one of the holiest mosques in all of Islam: the
Dome of the Rock in Jerusalem. Inflamed by these lies, an
armed Arab mob descended upon the New City of Jerusalem
on August 23, in an orgy of killing and looting. During the
following week the violence spread throughout the country,
very obviously organized and controlled from a single source.
In those places like Hebron and Safed, where the Jews were
caught unprepared, many perished. But in other areas, the
Jewish Self-Defense Forces (*Haganah*) checked the aggressors.
By the time British reinforcements, hurriedly rushed up from
Egypt, restored order, 133 Jews had been killed and 116 Arabs.
This Arab uprising had an important impact upon British
policy in the Holy Land.

The British immediately undertook two official investigations of conditions in Palestine. Both were whitewashes of British administrative blunders, both were replete with errors, omissions, and misinterpretations. They led to the issuance by the British Colonial Secretary, Lord Passfield, of an official White Paper on the entire subject of Palestine. In this White Paper, the British government stated that "the Jewish National Home is not meant to be the principal feature of the Mandate." Furthermore, *no more agricultural land would be sold to Jews, and Jewish immigration would be severely curtailed.* This was total repudiation, not only of the Balfour Declaration, but also of several treaties. The Arabs rejoiced. Evidently violence paid handsome dividends.

Once again Weizmann, Sokolow, and other Zionist leaders got busy. Soon the British government was inundated with protests from organizations and individuals (not all of them Jewish by any means) all over the world. Political leaders in Britain such as Austen Chamberlain, Stanley Baldwin, and Winston Churchill assailed what they called Britain's "gross betrayal." Lloyd George led an attack on the White Paper in Parliament. Bowing before this storm of indignation, British Prime Minister Ramsay MacDonald wrote a letter to Weizmann in which he "interpreted" the White Paper. It had all been a most unfortunate misunderstanding, it seemed. The Balfour Declaration would be honored; land would continue to be sold to Jews; immigration would not be arbitrarily restricted. The Arabs referred to this as "the black letter," since it nullified the victory they thought they'd won. Once again the vital importance of the Zionist movement and its leadership *outside* Palestine was demonstrated. Great Britain would never have bowed to appeals from the Jews of Palestine; they were, after all, merely one of the subject colonial peoples

within the empire. But the British had to listen when the
Zionist voice spoke from Paris, New York, Washington — and
London itself.

It was under the shadow of these events that the Seventeenth World Zionist Congress met at Basel in July, 1931. It
seemed to many delegates that Weizmann's leadership was to
blame for the trouble in Palestine. It had all been due to
Weizmann's reliance on Britain's good intentions. But intentions, good or bad, provided no defense against raging Arab
mobs. Only a better-armed Haganah (in defiance of British
laws) could do that. Furthermore, Weizmann's enlarged Jewish Agency had proved to be a failure. It had enlisted no real,
practical support among non-Zionists — and financial contributions from America had dwindled to a trickle. Although it
was manifestly unfair to blame all this on Weizmann, the opposition to his leadership had grown bitter. While he still
commanded the support of a majority of the delegates, his
position was so seriously undermined that he decided to step
down as president of the World Zionist Organization. He was
succeeded in that post by Nahum Sokolow.

While most of the world was going through the somber pain
of the Great Depression, Palestine began to prosper. By the
end of 1931 there was a labor shortage, and beginning in 1932
the flow of immigration rose to new heights. This was, after
all, a pioneer country — everything had yet to be built, opportunity was everywhere. Of course, economic progress in
Palestine owed little to the British administration there. Jewish immigration continued to be capriciously restricted, and
no state lands were "found available" for Jewish settlement. A
sudden concern was expressed by the British over the fate of
Arab peasants "displaced" by Jewish colonization. A Royal
Commission was appointed to investigate this matter. Unfortunately, after two years of diligent search, only 665 "dis-

placed" Arabs could be found — and they had been hand-
somely paid for their lands by the new Jewish owners. A sum
of £250,000 was made available by the British to compensate
"displaced" Arabs — but only 43 such persons ever came forward to claim a share of the money. The truth was that Jewish
enterprise in Palestine had resulted in the "placing" of many
thousands of hitherto impoverished Arabs. So well were Arabs
doing in Palestine that many thousands made their way there
from the neighboring Arab states of Lebanon, Syria, and
Transjordan.

The Eighteenth Zionist Congress, which met in Prague at
the end of August, 1933, was embittered by the ongoing struggle between those who favored a frontal political assault
against the British administration in Palestine and those who
urged continued cooperation. And, too, while Palestine was
enjoying a measure of prosperity, the Zionist world movement,
suffering from the effects of the depression, was reduced to
near bankruptcy; its budget for the coming year would be less
than one million dollars, the lowest on record. But the congress of 1933 was faced with a much graver threat than par-
tisanship or poverty. For in January of that year Adolf Hitler
had come to power in Germany. His brown-shirted Storm
Troopers thundered through the streets of Berlin, Frankfurt,
Nuremburg, Hamburg, and all the cities and towns of what he
called his Third Reich. Although the world could not yet believe that he intended the mass extermination of all Jews, it
was clear that the 650,000 German Jews now faced a deadly
peril. Those who could, began to flee. But where could they
go? No country would accept them — not France, England, or
the United States. Only Palestine promised refuge. Ironically,
German Jews had been second only to Americans in placing
their faith in assimilation and opposing Zionism. Now it was
only Zionism that could save them.

166 # 166 NEXT YEAR IN JERUSALEM

So began the Fifth Aliyah. In 1934 42,000 new immigrants arrived in Palestine; in 1935, 62,000. About half of them came from Poland, where official harassment had reduced the Jewish community to poverty; the other half were fleeing for their very lives from Nazi Germany. There, the enactment of the infamous Nuremburg Laws in September, 1935, subjected all Jews to forced labor, stripped them of their German citizenship, forced them back into ghettoes, and even made them wear the yellow patch again. Overnight, German Jewry was reduced to living in medieval conditions — and it was clear that worse was to follow. Zionists around the world pleaded with the British government to allow increased Jewish immigration into the Holy Land. But the British, for reasons we will examine later, continued to turn a deaf ear. In the face of the mounting Nazi threat, the Nineteenth World Congress, which met at Lucerne at the end of August, 1935, once again closed ranks. Chaim Weizmann was again elected president of the World Zionist Organization, while Sokolow became honorary president.

By 1936 the Jewish population of Palestine numbered more than 200,000. Tel Aviv was now a city of 100,000. A new port had been opened at Haifa, and a pipeline from Iraq was bringing oil to its refineries. Outside the Old City of Jerusalem a New City was now rising, with modern residential quarters and handsome new buildings to house the Knesset. New agricultural settlements were springing up throughout the country — and the government could even boast a treasury surplus in 1936 of some £6,000,000.

All this work of reclamation, this modernization, this ferment of activity represented no threat to the Arab masses in Palestine. On the contrary; it offered opportunity. Many thousands of Arabs were employed in Jewish undertakings, many thousands were receiving a practical education in the ways of the modern, Western world. The Jews were communicating to them something of their own restless, dynamic spirit; they were beginning to question the exploitive social system under which they had always lived. This new ferment among their subjects was a threat not only to such Palestinian Arab leaders as the Grand Mufti of Jerusalem, but also to the rulers of Arab states beyond Palestine. These rulers derived their wealth and power from a feudal social system, unchanged for a thousand years, which rested on the poverty of masses of wretched Arab *fellaheen* (peasants). Jewish influence was now beginning to stir those masses from their age-old stagnation. By 1936 the Arab leaders decided to act. And they had new allies.

The so-called Arab Revolt, which began in 1936, received large material and moral support from Nazi Germany and Fascist Italy. Both Hitler and Mussolini, eager to undermine Britain's imperial position, found the Arab world a promising field of operations. The European dictators and the Arabs shared common enemies — the Allied democracies and the Jews. Hitler's successful defiance of the Western democracies and Mussolini's easy conquest of Abyssinia in the face of British and French diplomatic opposition dealt a serious blow to Allied prestige in the Arab world. In Egypt and Syria, Arab independence movements began, in 1936, to demand the expulsion of British and French forces — and in Palestine Arab leaders felt that their big chance had come.

The revolt began on April 19, 1936, with mob attacks on Jews in Jaffa. The violence soon spread throughout the country. Bands of armed Arabs descended on Jewish settlements, killing and destroying. Not only Jews were attacked this time; British garrison forces were also assaulted, and Arabs who refused to pay tribute to the marauding bands were murdered. A guerrilla war developed in which thousands of Jews, Britons, and Arabs were to lose their lives during the next three years.

The British rushed reinforcements to Palestine, but their measures remained halfhearted. It was not until September, 1937, when Arab guerrillas assassinated the British District Commissioner of Galilee, that the English began arresting some of the Arab leaders of the revolt. The chief of these, the Grand Mufti of Jerusalem, escaped into Lebanon — where he continued to direct guerrilla operations. With arms and money supplied by German and Italian agents, the Arabs achieved some notable successes. In the fall of 1938 the British were driven from several towns and villages and from most of the Old City of Jerusalem. Weeks of hard fighting were required to regain control.

Why did the British not use their ample forces to simply crush the revolt? Because British policy toward the Arabs from 1936 to 1939 was conditioned by events in Europe, not Palestine. In Europe, Britain and France were facing the deadliest peril in their entire history. A mightily rearmed Nazi Germany, led by the self-proclaimed world conqueror, Adolf Hitler, in combination with a newly-militant Fascist Italy, led by the swaggering Benito Mussolini, threatened war — a war for which the Allies were not prepared. Allied policy, largely in the hands of British Prime Minister Neville Chamberlain, was to buy time by appeasing the dictators. Time for Britain and France to rearm, time perhaps for Hitler (they hoped) to turn his wrath away from the democracies and toward the Soviet Union. The democratic governments of Austria, Spain, and Czechoslovakia were all betrayed by Chamberlain's appeasement policy — and so, too, were the Jews' hopes for a "National Home." With their empire in dire peril, the British now, more than ever, felt they could not risk the enmity of the Arab world beyond Palestine — nor the security of the vital imperial lifeline through the Suez Canal. Just as they had appeased Hitler, so too the British were prepared to appease the

Arab leaders of the Palestine revolt. In both cases their policy would prove to be tragically mistaken.

With British forces seeking to avoid combat against the Arabs in Palestine, the defense of the Jewish community there devolved almost entirely upon the Jewish self-defense forces — the Haganah. It now numbered some 25,000 volunteers and its units patrolled roads and protected cities, towns, villages, and farms. It was faced not only with military problems, but also with a grave moral question. The Arabs burned crops and groves of trees, blasted vehicles on the roads, shot down farmers in their fields, killed men, women, and children indiscriminately. Should the Jews retaliate in kind? Their answer was No. They followed, instead, the policy of *havlaga* (self-restraint), refusing to make innocent Arabs suffer with the guilty. They would not retaliate — only defend themselves.

Within the Haganah, the Jewish motorcycle squads were a unique force. They were trained in commando tactics by Captain Orde Charles Wingate — a remarkable Christian Englishman who was also an ardent Zionist. (Later, he would apply the tactics he developed in Palestine against the Japanese in Burma — with great success.)

The ordeal lasted three years. Of the many settlements which were attacked by the Arabs not one was lost or abandoned — in fact, fifty new settlements were created during those years. The Jewish population of Palestine rose to more than 475,000 — despite continuing immigration restrictions. While the Arabs uprooted 200,000 trees, more than a million new ones were planted. Large-scale irrigation projects had now turned the hills and fields of Judea green again — as they had been in the time of the Prophets. It was becoming apparent that with or without British protection, the Jews of Palestine were not about to be driven into the sea.

To all of this the British responded with yet another Royal

Commission of inquiry and yet another White Paper in 1937. This one advocated partition of Palestine between Jews and Arabs. The Jews might have accepted this solution (though the area to be allocated them was small) but they were not given the opportunity — for the Arabs would not hear of it. British politicians returned to their drawing boards and in 1939 came up with the idea that Arabs and Jews should confer in London with the British government to decide the future of Palestine. The Jews sent representatives to the London conference — but Arab representatives refused to sit with them at the same table. British Prime Minister Chamberlain was reduced to acting as a messenger boy carrying Arab demands to the Jews and their responses back to the Arabs. Despite the total lack of success of this so-called conference at which no one would confer, the British, in May, 1939, issued still another White Paper on Palestine.

This final document in the long series of British policy statements was all but an unconditional surrender to Arab demands. The mandate would be ended in ten years, at which time Palestine would become an independent nation. For the first five of the ten years, Jewish immigration into Palestine would continue under severe restrictions; after that time it would depend on Arab wishes. The purchase of any more land by Jews would also be severely restricted. Of course, the new state of Palestine envisaged in the White Paper would have a huge majority of Arab inhabitants — would, in fact, be an Arab state. The Balfour promise of a National Home for the Jewish people was thereby finally, formally buried.

The Arabs were satisfied with this document. Within a few weeks they ended their revolt. In that respect it may be said that the British appeasement policy in the Near East finally achieved its desired aim. When, a few months later, Britain plunged into the Second World War, the Arabs would at least remain neutral, and the Suez Canal lifeline would remain fairly secure.

All this was at the expense of Jewish hopes and dreams. Led by Winston Churchill, British politicians in Parliament denounced Chamberlain's White Paper as "shameful." The League of Nations declared that Britain could not so abuse its mandate. And the Twenty-first Zionist World Congress, meeting in Geneva in August, 1939, denounced it. Yet despite this betrayal, Weizmann proclaimed that all Jews, Zionist or not, must stand in the face of the coming Nazi onslaught in support of Britain and France. They were democracies where alone human decency might survive. "Their concern is ours," Weizmann declared, "their fight is our fight." A few days after these words were spoken, the Nazi hordes swarmed across the frontiers of Poland, and Zionism, caught in a world upheaval, entered its era of supreme struggle.

Haggada:

Pioneering

"We at Sejera [Ilaniyyah], therefore, responsible for our own defense, were always conscious of the possibility of attack. This sometimes led to over-vigilance — and to an amusing incident which is still fresh in my mind after fifty-eight years. I had been sowing a field rather far from our base at Sejera, and it was getting rather late. . . . I decided it was prudent to return home. . . . I took my mule and off I went. . . . Suddenly I heard shots coming from Sejera. . . . I raced back as fast as I could. As I approached the farm compound, I heard someone shout, 'Look, he's here.' The group then rushed up to me with cries of 'Where is he? Where's the bedouin? What happened? Did you kill him?'

"When they had calmed down, I heard the story. Some time after I left, they spotted a horse running riderless in the dusk. They immediately thought that since I had been gone so long . . . I must have been stopped by a bedouin who had no doubt dismounted in order to rob me. There must have been a fight, and the horse had made off — the horse they had seen. But they had not known whether I had killed the bedouin or the bedouin had killed me. . . .

"As they were telling me the story, one of them cried: 'Heavens above, it's MY horse!' In the general panic, none had recognized it. They had been so anxious about the delay in my return that they had imagined an attack. . . .

> — *David Ben-Gurion,*
> *from* Ben-Gurion
> Looks Back

9

Holocaust

Happy is the match consumed igniting the flame;
Happy is the flame ablaze in the heart's recess;
Happy is the heart in honor beating at last:
Happy is the match consumed igniting the flame.
                                        HANNAH SENESCH

The story has been told before. It has been told in fiction and
poetry and diaries and the documents of governments and the
testimony heard in a hundred courtrooms. But the terrible
nightmare a world would like to forget must be told anew in
every generation so that the story never passes into myth. For
the things we are about to record really happened; they happened to real men, women, and children and they happened
within the memory of the living.

Between September, 1939, when Nazi Germany conquered
Poland, and May, 1945, when Adolf Hitler's "Thousand-Year
Reich" came tumbling down in ruins, more than six million
human beings whose only "offense" was the fact that they were
Jews were systematically murdered in Nazi-dominated Europe.
In 1946, just before he was hanged for the killing of hundreds
of thousands of people — Jews and non-Jews alike, Hans
Frank, the Nazi governor general of Poland, declared: "A
thousand years will pass and the guilt of Germany will not be
erased." He was right. But, as we shall see, he was not inclusive

enough — for the guilt was not only Germany's but, to a large extent, the world's.

With Adolf Hitler, hatred of Jews assumed the depth and malignancy of a psychosis. During his rise to power in Germany, he had used anti-Semitism as one of his chief weapons. The Jews, he shrieked, were responsible for Germany's defeat in 1918; the Jews had brought about the Great Depression; the Jews were bloated, superrich capitalists; the Jews were scheming, revolutionary Communists; the Jews were untiring enemies of the entire human race. These barbarous and idiotic ideas were fervently embraced by many millions of Germans (and some non-Germans) who were eager to blame the traditional scapegoat for all the economic, political, and social woes that world war, depression, and industrialization had brought upon European society. The anti-Semitic heritage of the Christian world made a fertile soil for Hitler's seeds of hatred. The war he waged against civilization was not merely one of political and geographical conquest; one of its chief aims was the absolute extermination of the entire Jewish race.

Hitler's first victims were the German Jews, stripped of their citizenship and reduced to medieval conditions by the infamous Nuremburg Laws of 1935. Thousands were murdered by Hitler's Storm Troopers and by anti-Semitic German mobs during the early years of the Nazi dictatorship; many thousands more were imprisoned in concentration camps, where death came more slowly but no less surely. Those who could, fled — leaving behind them all their worldly possessions. When Hitler first came to power in Germany, in 1933, there were some 650,000 German Jews. By the beginning of the war in 1939 that number had shrunk to fewer than 250,000. At war's end in 1945 there would be fewer than 50,000 left alive.

But it was not until after the war began that the Nazis began their systematic campaign of liquidation. As the German

armies swept into Poland in 1939 and Russia in 1941, they
were followed by special murder squads composed of fanatical
SS men. These units, the infamous *Einsatz Kommandos,*
would round up all the Jews and machine-gun them to death.
Some were killed in special gas vans. The bodies were tossed
into huge mass graves previously dug by the victims themselves. It has been estimated that two million Jews in Poland
and Russia perished at the hands of the SS death commandos.

But the work of the Einsatz Kommandos was not efficient
enough to bring about what Hitler referred to as "the final
solution to the Jewish problem" throughout conquered Europe. A more systematic method was necessary. So, with typical
German thoroughness, several special Extermination Centers
were built, mostly in Poland, and their names — Maidanek,
Treblinka, Sobibor, Auschwitz, and many others — have become symbols of bestiality. In Auschwitz alone six thousand
people a day were murdered and cremated.

The annihilation pattern was everywhere the same. First, all
the Jews of a given area would be driven into squalid ghettoes
where their morale was systematically undermined. Set apart
from the rest of a conquered population, they were told that
they were to be "resettled" in the east. They would be
rounded up and marched to the local freight train yards.
There they would be herded into boxcars and shipped to Poland or other occupied centers. When the trains, after long
journeys during which no food or water was provided, arrived
at Auschwitz or some other Extermination Center, the surviving travelers would be gathered together at the railroad siding.
There Nazi doctors would examine them. Those who were
judged fit for labor were marched away, never to be seen
again. Every attempt was made to fool the victims into thinking they would, at least, survive. Picture postcards were
handed out to be signed and mailed back to friends and rela-

tives; sometimes an orchestra (made up of concentration camp inmates) played. Then the Jews were marched over to large structures surrounded by well-kept lawns and flower gardens, which bore signs reading "Baths." The men, women, and children were made to undress and told they were about to take a shower. Then they were packed into the "shower room" — two thousand at a time — and the doors were locked and hermetically sealed. And while the victims looked up and wondered why no water came from the "shower spouts," crystals of deadly hydrogen cyanide gas were poured into the vents. It usually took half an hour for the people inside to die. At the end of that time the gas chambers would be opened and men wearing gas masks would enter to remove the gold teeth from the corpses and cut off their hair (which was useful to the German economy). Then the bodies were carted over to specially designed crematoriums, where they were incinerated.

And what of those Jews who had been selected for labor rather than the gas chambers on arrival? They were first worked to exhaustion in war plants set up near the Extermination Camps — and then sent to the gas chambers. There was no escape — not even for infants. Of the six million Jews killed in Europe, it has been estimated that one million were small children. "The Nazi conspirators," said the formal indictment brought against them at the Nuremburg trials, "mercilessly destroyed even children. They killed them with their parents, in groups and alone. They killed them in children's homes and hospitals, burying the living in the graves, throwing them into flames, stabbing them with bayonets, poisoning them, conducting experiments upon them, extracting their blood for the use of the German army, throwing them into prison and Gestapo torture chambers and concentration camps, where the children died from hunger, torture and epidemic diseases."

The extermination campaign was generally carried out on a

national basis — one country at a time. Thus most of the Jews
in Poland were destroyed before the Nazis turned to France,
thence to Belgium, Holland, Hungary, and so on. As the Nazis
themselves admitted, this stupendous campaign of mass murder could not have been carried out without the cooperation
or, at least, the passive neutrality of the great majority of non-
Jewish citizens of the conquered countries. Proof of this is the
fact that in those places where the people resisted Hitler's
"final solution to the Jewish problem," the extermination
program was unsuccessful — as in Denmark and Bulgaria,
Despite the many instances of help extended them by Christian neighbors in other lands, by and large the Jews of Europe
found themselves alone — utterly alone — in the face of the
Nazi hordes.

Alone they suffered and alone they fought back. For there
were uprisings in the ghettoes of Wilno, Bialystok, Bedzin,
Krakow, Tarnopol, Czestochowa, and Stry. There were even
revolts in the murder camps of Sobibor, Treblinka, and
Auschwitz. In the spring of 1943 the Warsaw Ghetto rose, and
the almost unarmed, starving, and disease-ridden inhabitants
held off the German forces for several days before perishing in
the ruins of their city-within-a-city. Through luck and incred-
ible courage some survived these uprisings — some even escaped the death camps and made their way to Palestine.

What of the western democracies, England and the United
States? Could they do nothing to prevent this mass murder or
to save some, at least, of its victims? Gestures were made. As
early as 1938 President Franklin D. Roosevelt had initiated a
conference on the subject of saving German Jews from Hitler's
fury. Thirty-two countries sent representatives to Evian in
France to consider the matter. Many speeches were made. But
no country would change its immigration laws in ways that
would permit the entry of those thousands of German Jews

seeking refuge. Indeed, in that same year Hitler announced
that any German Jew who wished could leave Germany (pro-
viding he left all his worldly goods behind). Many, many
thousands tried to take advantage of this momentary release.
They crowded the German port cities of Bremen and Hamburg, but they had no place to go. Even when some few of
them boarded ships, these ships had no real destination. One
group sailed completely around the world — touching at the
United States, South American countries, and even Australia.
They were not permitted to land and, eventually, were returned to Hamburg and certain death. They could not land in
Palestine because they were not part of the small quota of
Jewish immigrants that Britain would permit to enter each
year. And after war broke out Britain would permit no German Jews at all to enter Palestine because they were "enemy
aliens"! A British ordinance published soon after war began
even barred Palestine to all Jews from territory *held* by the
Germans — which meant all of conquered Europe.

There were expressions of sympathy and indignation in the
United States: public demonstrations, congressional resolutions, and so on. And in April, 1943, representatives of Britain
and the United States met at Bermuda to see if they could
devise some measures for saving the doomed. But the delegates
to the Bermuda Conference found insuperable obstacles in
American immigration laws, the scarcity of shipping, and —
the British White Paper on Palestine of 1939. In January of
1944, Roosevelt established a War Refugees Board "to forestall the plan of the Nazis to exterminate all the Jews and
other persecuted minorities in Europe." The word "forestall"
was a bitter mockery; the extermination campaign had been in
progress for years and its victims already numbered millions.
The board, with the help of the Jewish Agency, did establish
an office in Turkey — and did save some hundreds of Jewish

lives. There were also attempts by American undercover agencies, such as the Office of Strategic Services (OSS), to trade trucks and other war matériel to the Germans in return for Jewish lives — but none of these "deals" came to fruition.

While these halfhearted and feeble gestures were being made by the Allied governments, daring efforts were made by Palestinian Jews and various Zionist groups throughout Europe to rescue as many victims as possible. Palestinian agents established contact with Jewish partisan groups in Nazi-occupied countries, helped smuggle refugees across borders, provided them with false papers, and smuggled them onto ships for the hazardous voyage to Palestine. Hundreds of these ships — small, broken-down coastal freighters for the most part, called "coffin ships" — made their way from ports in unoccupied France, Greece, and even Italy to the coast of the Holy Land. Though many were intercepted by the British and their human cargo interned or deported, some tens of thousands of European Jews were saved in this way — but the number was a pitiful fraction of those being slaughtered. Not only did those Palestinian Jews who pierced the Nazi wall of blood and terror save lives — their mere presence brought spiritual hope to the forgotten and condemned prisoners of the ghettoes.

One of the boldest rescue missions undertaken by the Jews of Palestine was that of a group of 32 agents who were parachuted behind enemy lines in Yugoslavia in the spring of 1944. Their task was to help save as many Hungarian and Romanian Jews as possible (most had already perished). They helped several thousand Jews to escape the Nazis — and they also established Jewish partisan groups behind Nazi lines and helped large numbers of downed American airmen to escape the Germans. But, in their own words, the greatest service they rendered their people was "the mere fact of our presence."

One of those who parachuted into Nazi-occupied Yugoslavia in 1944 was the young poet (she was twenty-three years old) Hannah Senesch. She had come to Palestine from Hungary in 1939 and later worked in the fishing and farming kibbutz of Sedot Yam (Seafields). Her mission was to organize the rescue of Jewish children from Hungary. She was betrayed to the Nazis by some Hungarian peasants. For five months she underwent every kind of Nazi torture without revealing to her captors the purpose of her mission. She was condemned to death. Asked if she wished to plead for mercy, she replied, "I ask for no mercy from hangmen." She refused a blindfold when she was shot to death in the prison courtyard.

It has been estimated that some fifty thousand European Jews were saved from the Nazis by Palestinian agents — less than one percent of those murdered — but only from Palestine was any organized attempt at all made to save even that fraction.

It was the *fighting* front to which the Jews of Palestine most wished to be sent. They yearned to fight the Nazis face-to-face. When, in September, 1939, the British issued a call for volunteers, more than 136,000 men and women of the Jewish community in Palestine responded — more than a quarter of the entire population! The British accepted these volunteers into both combat and noncombatant units — but with an important reservation. The Jewish volunteers were not to be identified as Jews — but as Palestinians. It would not do, the British felt, to allow Jews as Jews to make too great a contribution to the common struggle — for that might have political implications after the war. In the so-called Palestine Regiment that was raised, every Jewish unit was supposed to be matched by an Arab unit. Unfortunately, this did not work out — almost no Arabs volunteered. Nonetheless, in dispatches and news releases, Jews fighting the Germans in North Africa,

Greece, Syria, Abyssinia, and the many other places they served were referred to always as Palestinians — with the clear implication that they might well be Arabs. Not until 1944 was a Jewish brigade, fighting under its own flag, allowed to be identified. This brigade fought through the bitter Italian campaign and gave a good account of itself against the Nazi "supermen." They fought their way into Austria and, by war's end in 1945, were bivouacked in Belgium and Holland. Needless to say, these soldiers used every opportunity to help save surviving Jews in the areas through which they campaigned. The mere sight of their uniform and flag, the blue and white flag of Zion, gave a thrill of hope to the despairing.

If the British refused, for so long, to identify Jewish units for fear of offending the Arabs and of strengthening the moral claim of Jews to their National Home in Palestine, it was because they had no fear of offending Jewish feelings; the Jews would fight Hitler, in any event. Instead, Britain bent her efforts to appease and mollify the Arabs of Palestine and the Near East, but without much success. Very few Arabs fought on Britain's side. The Arabs of Iraq staged a pro-Nazi rebellion in 1941 under the leadership of the Grand Mufti of Jerusalem, who called for a Holy War against the Allies. In Egypt, only the British Army prevented a pro-German takeover. In Syria, the leading Arab political parties were in the pay of Nazi agents. After the revolt in Iraq was crushed, the Grand Mufti of Jerusalem fled to Italy and then to Berlin, where he served Hitler faithfully, broadcasting Nazi propaganda to the Moslem world, recruiting Moslem forces for the Germans, and acting as an advisor in the task of murdering European Jews.

Just as the Jewish people perished before the onslaught of the Nazi terror in Europe, so too, did the organized Zionist movement in Europe. The entire Jewish communities of

Poland, Germany, and White Russia, which had always been in the forefront of Zionist activity, were destroyed. Although individual Zionists and small groups were prominent in all the European resistance movements, fighting an underground war against the Nazis in every conquered nation, Europe could never again be an important reservoir of Zionist strength. It was up to American Jews now to assume the burdens of leadership. Indeed, the American Jewish community, which numbered some five million, was now the largest single surviving body of Jews anywhere in the world.

The onslaught of Nazism did much to close the ranks of American Zionists. With the outbreak of war in 1939, the arguments which had divided the followers of Louis Brandeis from the main Zionist organization faded away. And, as the war progressed and the terrible agony of European Jewry became ever clearer, American Jews who had opposed Zionism began to see that assimilation had done nothing to save the Jews of Europe; no matter how "French," "German," "Polish," "Hungarian," or "Romanian" the Jews of those countries had considered themselves to be, their enemies had singled them out as a separate race, an alien entity to be destroyed. And the Christian governments of Europe and the world had done little or nothing to save them, their own "citizens." The old argument that Zionism involved Jews in a kind of "double loyalty" rang very hollow in the face of the holocaust.

The immediate response of American Zionists to the onslaught of war was to set up an emergency committee for Zionist affairs. In January, 1942, that committee became the American Zionist Emergency Council, which became the executive arm of the movement in America and, to a large extent, of the entire world. The council began its career under the leadership of Rabbi Stephen Wise; in 1943 Abba Hillel

Silver became cochairman. The council's function was to act as the spokesman of Zionism in the United States, the country whose influence might well prove decisive for the future of Palestine. It was essential, therefore, to win public opinion in America for the Zionist solution. In pursuit of that objective the council was tireless. More than four hundred local emergency councils were established. Forty state legislatures were persuaded to adopt pro-Zionist resolutions; forty state governors were induced to send pro-Zionist petitions to President Roosevelt. Leaders in every sphere — government, industry, labor, religion, education, and the arts — were drawn into the cause. Senator Robert Wagner of New York headed the American Palestine Committee, composed entirely of eminent Christians — some fifteen thousand of them. More than twenty-five hundred Christian clergymen joined the Christian Council of Palestine, headed by Henry A. Atkinson, leader of the Church Peace Union. Later these two groups would merge into the powerful American Christian Palestine Committee. At their annual conventions in 1944 both the A.F.L. and the C.I.O. voted to support the Zionist objectives in Palestine. In 1944 the campaign platforms of both the Republican and Democratic parties called for the establishment of a Jewish state in Palestine. American public opinion was won — not only by the tireless activity of American Zionists, but also by the mute and indescribably pitiful testimony of the suffering Jews of Europe. However feebly their government may have responded to the holocaust, the American people were not without a conscience.

The fearful example of the holocaust united American Jews as they had never been united before. The many organizations, both Jewish and Christian, such as the American Fund for Palestine, Brandeis's old Palestine Economic Corporation, the American Friends of the Hebrew University, the Ameri-

can Technion Society, the American Zionist Youth Commission, Avukah (later the Intercollegiate Zionist Federation),
Hadassah, B'nai B'rith, the Labor Zionist Organization, and,
of course, the central group, the Zionist Organization of
America, could count an organized membership of more than
one million — and the real membership, if indirect affiliations
were counted, was more than two million. Even those wealthy
Jews who still held aloof from the Zionist dream did not now
withhold their money.

The United Palestine Appeal joined in a common effort
with other leading Jewish organizations to finance relief and
rehabilitation work overseas. They formed a new instrument,
the United Jewish Appeal, which in the single year 1947 received in voluntary donations the sum of $170,000,000. That
amount of money would have seemed fabulous to Herzl — he
would have considered it more than sufficient to bring all his
hopes to fruition. This nationwide fundraising effort was led
by Henry Morgenthau, Jr., no longer U.S. Ambassador to
Turkey but for many years now Secretary of the Treasury.

American Zionists did not limit themselves to funding,
however. They also actively demonstrated against Great Britain's Palestinian policy as expressed in the infamous White
Paper of 1939. That policy was literally killing Jews by the
hundreds of thousands by denying them refuge from the Nazi
horror. In a conference which took place in May, 1942, at New
York's Hotel Biltmore, the White Paper of 1939 was denounced as having "no legal or moral validity." At another
conference held in New York in September, 1943 — a conference whose delegates represented directly or indirectly more
than two and a half million American citizens — a declaration
was issued which stated: "We call for the fulfillment of the
Balfour Declaration . . . to reconstitute Palestine as the Jewish
Commonwealth."

It was American money which purchased and outfitted the coffin ships in which Jews fleeing the Nazi terror sought refuge in Palestine, and all during the war years a strange battle of immigration was waged between the Zionist movement and Great Britain. Strange because, on the one hand, Jews in Palestine and all over the world were actively and enthusiastically fighting alongside Britain against Nazism — but against the British policy in the Holy Land. As David Ben-Gurion said, referring to the battle against the White Paper of 1939: "We will fight the war as if there were no White Paper, and we will fight the White Paper as if there were no war."

The Battle of Immigration continued to be fought in the port cities of many lands and on many seas. A far-flung network of Jewish and Zionist agents was created to buy old ships (any seaworthy ships during the war years were already impressed into Allied service), assemble refugees, conduct them on their perilous journey out of Hitler's Europe, and transport them to Palestine. Against this rescue effort the British threw their naval and air forces in the Mediterranean, their military establishment in Palestine, and even their diplomats in neutral countries through which the fugitives might pass. It was perhaps the most inglorious war ever waged by the British Empire — every British victory was a tragedy.

Through the daring efforts of Palestinian agents such as the poet Hannah Senesch, Jewish refugees were conducted along dangerous underground routes and gathered in Mediterranean and Black Sea ports. There they embarked at night upon their derelict vessels (some of them riverboats from America) and then set out for Palestine. Many such ships were captured by the British. When that happened the refugees were sent to detention camps on the disease-ridden prison island of Mauritius in the Indian Ocean. Those ships which eluded the British blockade of Palestine landed their human cargo on the beaches of the Holy Land, where detachments of the Haganah brought them to land, sometimes wading out to the ship and carrying the refugees ashore on their shoulders. Then these "illegal" immigrants would be dispersed swiftly among the various Jewish settlements. Of course, the British Army regularly raided settlements suspected of harboring "illegals." But what could a British officer do when, after assembling all the inhabitants of a settlement in order to weed out "illegals," he found that not one of those assembled had identity papers?

The coffin ships had begun to arrive off Palestine as early as 1939. Even on the day the war started, one of them, the *Tiger Hill*, was fired upon by the British and three of her passengers were killed. But the ships kept coming. Some achieved bitter renown. One was the *Salvador*, which, with 350 refugees aboard, sailed from Bulgaria and reached Istanbul in December, 1940. Since they had no papers, the *Salvador*'s passengers were not permitted to land. The ship put back into the Black Sea, where it was overwhelmed by a storm. Two hundred thirty of the refugees aboard drowned. In March, 1941, the *Darien* reached Haifa in sinking condition. Her 800 passengers were allowed to land, but were immediately marched off to a British internment camp. In November, 1940, the *Atlantic* arrived at Haifa with some 1,900 refugees from Hitler. They were imprisoned by the British for two weeks and then shipped out again to Mauritius. Another group of nearly 2,000 "illegals" was shipped out to Mauritius by the British in November, 1940, aboard the British vessel *Patria*. But some among her long-suffering passengers must have resolved to bring their hopeless journey to an end. They blew up the *Patria* in Haifa harbor; 260 perished. In December of 1942 a leaky old hulk called the *Struma*, with 769 Jewish refugees aboard, half of them women and children, arrived at Istanbul. The Turks refused to let the passengers land — they had no valid permits to proceed to Palestine. For two months the *Struma,* her passengers packed aboard, waited in the harbor at Istanbul while the Zionist Organization in Palestine pleaded desperately with the British to grant them entry permits — if not all, then some — at least the children. Finally the Turkish authorities ordered the *Struma* to depart. A short distance from harbor she broke up and sank, and all but one of her pitiful cargo went down with her. These are but a few examples of the tragedies of the Battle of Immigration. Many ships went down, many refugees perished — but many others, miraculously, completed their journey.

When, after 1943, the defeat of Germany appeared certain, the war between Britian and Zionism became more stubborn and savage. Neither side called it war. The Jews of Palestine called it resistance; the British called it a campaign to suppress terrorism. Their aim was to suppress and to disarm the Haganah. The British maintained that the Jews of Palestine should depend on the British army and police for protection against Arab attacks; the Jews knew that would be suicidal. So the British conducted constant raids to seize Haganah supply dumps and capture Haganah leaders. They made no such exertions against Arabs.

It was against this desperate background that a new note was sounded by a minority of Palestinian Jews: the note of terrorism. To Arab attacks and to British raids, even when Jewish lives were lost, as they so often were, the Haganah and the Zionist leadership had always refused to retaliate in kind. They would fight in self-defense, but they would not kill Arabs or British soldiers for vengeance. But as early as 1938, some members of Haganah could no longer accept this strict discipline. They seceded from that organization to form themselves into the *Irgun Zvai Leumi* (the National Military Organization).

The Irgun, convinced that the British would never leave Palestine until they had been blown out, engaged in destroying British military installations. They always warned British personnel to evacuate these places before they were attacked — but their warnings were sometimes too late. Such tactics, which were frowned upon by the Haganah, were not yet violent enough for some Irgunists. In 1943 a handful of them, led by Abraham Stern, formed their own terrorist group, known as the Stern Gang. The Sternists, whose leader was shot and killed by the British in 1944, committed acts of terror without restraint or warning.

In 1943 and 1944 Irgunists began blowing up British police stations in Palestine. In August, 1944, Sternists attempted (unsuccessfully) to assassinate the British High Commissioner, Sir Harold MacMichael. It was Sir Harold who had condemned the *Struma* passengers to death by refusing all pleas to grant them entrance permits. In November, 1944, two Sternists traveled to Cairo, where they killed Lord Moyne, the British Resident Minister in the Middle East. Haganah leaders, Palestinian Jews, and Zionists the world over denounced these crimes as not only immoral, but dangerous to the cause of Zionism. For more than a year the Haganah devoted a considerable amount of its energies to catching these terrorists and turning them over to the British authorities who — ironically — were attempting to stamp out the Haganah! Terrorism, a mode of warfare so utterly repugnant to Jewish ideals and beliefs, was condemned by the majority. As for the minority who practiced it, their madness is at least understandable when measured against the terrible sufferings of the holocaust and a blind British policy which threatened to turn the promised Jewish National Home in Palestine into a Jewish ghetto in an Arab world.

And, finally, in May of 1945, the long nightmare in Europe

came to its end. Hitler was dead, Germany crushed. The advancing armies had uncovered the extermination camps, to the horror of the civilized world. More than six million Jews had been killed — an ancient, colorful and deeply honorable culture, that of eastern European Jewry, had been wiped from the face of the earth. Only ashes remained. Ashes and a pitiful handful of one hundred thousand Jewish "displaced persons," survivors of the holocaust whom the Nazis, owing to the rapid advance of the liberating armies, had not had time to kill and who were still "living" in German concentration camps. These hundred thousand could not go back to the lands in which they had once lived; those lands were the terrible graveyards of everything they had known and loved. In many places the Nazi brand of anti-Semitism had infected local populations so that Jews were no longer welcome in their old homelands. Neither the United States nor any other nation was willing to admit them. Only in Palestine would they be welcome.

In July, 1945, a new government came to power in Britain; the British Labour Party had won the elections. This was the party which, in 1944, had declared: "There is surely neither hope nor meaning in a Jewish National Home unless we are prepared to let the Jews, if they wish, enter this tiny land in such numbers as to become a majority. There was a strong case for this before the war, and there is an irresistible case for it now, after the unspeakable atrocities of the cold-blooded, calculated German-Nazi plans to kill all the Jews of Europe." Surely now, British policy would undergo a change. Furthermore, the new American President, Harry S Truman, had publicly urged the British to throw open the gates of Palestine to the Hundred Thousand. In September, 1945, came the British response. The new Labour government offered 1,500 immigration certificates which were still available under the White Paper of 1939! This could be interpreted only as a

British declaration of war against Zionism. Millions of people throughout the world, of all political and religious beliefs, were shocked. How, in the light of all that had happened, could the British pursue so cruel a policy?

For the same old imperial reasons. Long before the war in Europe had ended, British Prime Minister Winston Churchill (himself a friend of Zionism) had stated: "I did not become His Majesty's First Minister in order to preside over the dissolution of the British Empire." Churchill was no longer Prime Minister — but the British Labour Party, upon assuming the reins of government, found that imperial responsibilities outweighed idealism and even simple human decency. The Arab world was large and potentially strong; Arab resources, especially oil, were huge and vital. Britain's war-torn economy demanded both the continued exploitation of Arab resources and of the wealth of whatever bits and pieces of the empire could still be held. Against these considerations the fate of the Jews in Palestine or of the Jewish survivors of the holocaust weighed little.

The war in Europe was over — but the war in Palestine would go on. Now it would enter its decisive phase.

Haggada:

Judgment at Nuremburg

In summing up the case against the surviving leaders of the Nazi German Government, on trial in 1946 for crimes against humanity, the chief British prosecutor, Sir Hartley Shawcross, read to the British, American, and Russian judges an eyewitness account of the mass murder of a Jewish community in Russia:

" 'Without screaming or weeping these people undressed, stood around in family groups, kissed each other, said farewells, and waited for a sign from another SS man, who stood near the pit, also with a whip in his hand. During the fifteen minutes that I stood near I heard no complaint or plea for mercy. I watched a family of about eight persons, a man and a woman, both about fifty with their children of about one, eight and nineteen and two grown-up daughters of about twenty–twenty-four. An old woman with snow-white hair was holding the one-year-old child in her arms and singing to it and tickling it. The child was cooing with delight. The couple were looking on with tears in their eyes. The father was holding the hand of a boy about ten years old and speaking to him softly; the boy was fighting his tears. The father pointed to the sky, stroked his head and seemed to explain something to him. At that moment the SS man at the pit shouted something to his comrade. The latter counted off about 20 persons and instructed them to go behind the earth mound. Among them was the family which I have mentioned. . . . I walked around the mound and found myself confronted by a tremendous grave. People were closely wedged together and lying on top of each other so that only their heads were visible . . . the pit was already two thirds full. I estimated that it already contained about 1,000 people. I looked for the man who did the shooting. He was an SS man who sat on the edge of the narrow end of the pit, his feet dangling into the pit. He had a tommy gun on his knees and was smoking a cigarette. . . . Then I heard a series of shots. . . .' "

Sir Hartley paused, then said: "You will remember this story when you come to give your decision, but not in vengeance — in a determination that these things shall not occur again. The father — you remember — pointed to the sky, and seemed to say something to his boy."

10

The State Is Reborn

The great historical phenomenon of the Jewish return is
unique because the position of the Jewish people as a homeless people, yet attached with an unbreakable tenacity to its
birthplace, is unique. It is that phenomenon which has made
the problem of Palestine an issue in international affairs, and
no similar problem has ever arisen.

MOSHE SHARETT

That Britain really meant to implement a postwar "get tough"
policy against the Jews of Palestine was demonstrated when, in
September, 1945, a large "show trial" got under way in Haifa.
There twenty Jews accused of possessing arms illegally were
condemned to various prison terms. The Jewish response was a
series of demonstrations throughout Palestine and the first
broadcast of Kol Israel (Voice of Israel), the secret, underground radio station of the Haganah, which hurled defiance
across the airways, stating that the gates of Palestine would be
held open for Jewish survivors of the holocaust. On the last
day of October, 1945, railway stations, bridges, and British
police boats in Haifa harbor were blown up by the Haganah.

Finally, on November 13, 1945, the British government,
through the voice of its Foreign Secretary, the portly Ernest
Bevin (former head of the British Transport and General
Workers Union — a man of stubborn will), declared that, instead of allowing the Hundred Thousand to proceed to Palestine, a new Commission of Inquiry would investigate matters.
This commission was to be composed of an equal number of

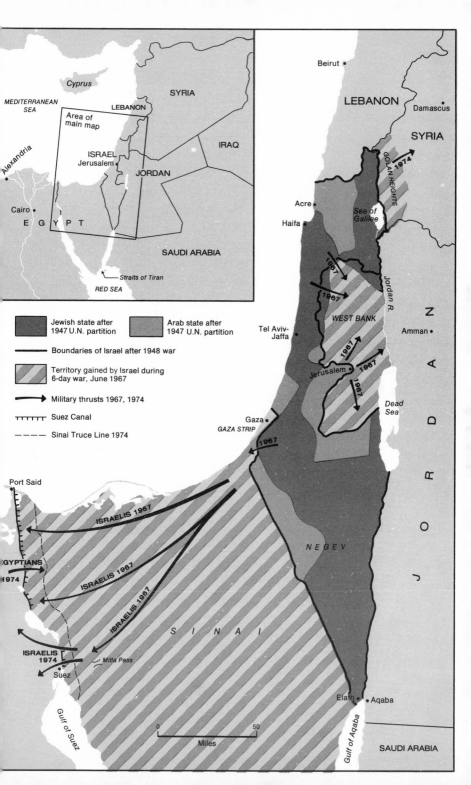

MEDITERRANEAN SEA

Cyprus

SYRIA

LEBANON

Area of main map

IRAQ

ISRAEL
Jerusalem

JORDAN

Alexandria

Cairo

E G Y P T

SAUDI ARABIA

Straits of Tiran

RED SEA

Beirut

LEBANON

Damascus

SYRIA

1974

Acre

Sea of Galilee

GOLAN HEIGHTS

Haifa

1967

1967

WEST BANK

Jordan R.

J O R D A N

Tel Aviv-Jaffa

Amman

1967

Jerusalem

1967

1967

Dead Sea

Gaza

GAZA STRIP

1967

Jewish state after 1947 U.N. partition

Arab state after 1947 U.N. partition

Boundaries of Israel after 1948 war

Territory gained by Israel during 6-day war, June 1967

Military thrusts 1967, 1974

Suez Canal

Sinai Truce Line 1974

Port Said

ISRAELIS 1967

N E G E V

EGYPTIANS
1974

ISRAELIS 1967

ISRAELIS 1967

S I N A I

ISRAELIS 1974

Mitla Pass

Suez

Elath

Aqaba

Gulf of Suez

Gulf of Aqaba

0   50
Miles

SAUDI ARABIA

Britons and Americans. Bevin even went so far as to admonish the survivors of the Nazi murder mills that their eagerness to get to Palestine might irritate the Christian world — "You have the danger of another anti-Semitic reaction through it all," he warned. In any event, Bevin promised to abide by the decision of the Commission of Inquiry.

The commission visited Palestine and also visited the Displaced Persons Camps in Europe. In April, 1946, it published its recommendations. It urged that the Hundred Thousand be admitted into Palestine immediately. The recommendations were unanimous. Would the British honor their promise now? No, they would not. In May, Prime Minister Attlee declared that in order to admit the Hundred Thousand Britain required American financial support. And furthermore, as a precondition to their admission, the Haganah must disarm and disband itself! Taking the initiative, British forces in Palestine, in June, 1946, arrested and interned 2,718 leaders of the Jewish community and officially outlawed the Jewish Agency. The arrests were followed by an offensive against the Haganah and the Irgun.

But the Haganah was ready. It immediately blew up the five bridges that spanned the Jordan River and disrupted the roads and railways of the country. When large British forces descended on settlements they were met with passive resistance — against which they were helpless. As tensions mounted, acts of terrorism on both sides multiplied. On July 22, 1946, the Irgun blew up the south wing of the King David Hotel in Jerusalem, killing nearly a hundred people, forty of them Jews. The wing was occupied by the British government secretariat — and the Irgun planned its destruction as a reprisal for the arrest of the Jewish Agency leaders. The Irgun had telephoned a warning first to evacuate the hotel, but the warning was ignored. There was an outbreak of protest among Jews all over Palestine against the Irgun for this action — but short of starting a civil war, there was little the Haganah could do to control the extremists.

In November, 1946, British police (some of whom were members of Sir Oswald Mosley's Union of British Fascists), maddened by Jewish resistance, lost all discipline on the streets of Tel Aviv and Jerusalem, firing into private houses and wounding scores of men, women, and children. In December the Irgun, retaliating for the flogging by the British of one of its members, kidnapped and flogged a British major and three sergeants. In January, 1947, the Irgun blew up police headquarters in Haifa and, a few days later, the British High Commissioner in Palestine ordered the evacuation of British women and children from the strife-torn country. By that time, Palestine had become a police state under martial law — but it was the British, more than the Jews, who found themselves in a state of siege.

The battle of immigration was also intensified. In the fall of 1945 the Haganah destroyed British coastal radar stations used to detect the approach of coffin ships. These desperate boatloads of refugees continued to arrive — some to land successfully, others to be sent to internment camps on Cyprus. The *Enzo Sereni,* with a thousand refugees aboard, was intercepted by the British in January, 1946; the *Four Freedoms,* with another thousand refugees, was boarded by the British in September, 1946. Only after a fierce struggle were her passengers subdued. The passengers of the *Palmach* (the ship was named after the special Haganah commando units) also resisted a British boarding party; one was killed and a hundred wounded in the fight.

It was under the shadow of this intensifying struggle that, after a lapse of seven years, the Twenty-second World Zionist Congress met in Basel, Switzerland, in 1946. Many were missing from the ranks. "It was a dreadful experience," recalled Chaim Weizmann, "to stand before that assembly and run one's eyes along row after row of delegates, finding among them hardly one of the friendly faces that had adorned past Congresses. Polish Jewry was missing; central and southeastern European Jewry was missing; German Jewry was missing." Gone were the representatives of six million people. And as a reminder of the precarious fate of the survivors of the Nazi murder mills, sixteen delegates from Displaced Persons Camps, in which the Hundred Thousand still waited, were present. Also attending were observers from the governments of the United States, the Soviet Union, and nearly a dozen other nations — but not Great Britain.

Great Britain had come up with still another "plan" for Palestine. Or rather "plans." The first was an offer to create a federated state of Palestine divided into Jewish and Arab cantons. The Hundred Thousand would be admitted into a tiny area of 1,400 square miles. The second, the Bevin Plan, called for the admission of the Hundred Thousand over a period of many years, to be followed by the establishment of Jewish and Arab semiautonomous zones in Palestine, all under British authority. Both plans were rejected by Jews and Arabs alike. At which point the British government invited both Jews and Arabs to confer in London on the entire matter.

So the World Zionist Congress was faced with two urgent questions. Should they accept any sort of plan that envisaged the partition of Palestine? Should they accept Britain's invitation to attend the London Conference? One group, headed by Weizmann and Rabbi Stephen Wise, answered yes to both questions. They still believed in some sort of accommodation with the British. But another group, led by Abba Hillel Silver and David Ben-Gurion, answered no. After a long and heated debate, the Silver–Ben-Gurion group won. The con-

gress officially demanded the immediate creation of a Jewish
state in Palestine and rejected the British invitation — calling
the Bevin Plan a "travesty of Britain's obligations under the
Mandate." Weizmann resigned the presidency of the congress
— but no new president was chosen. Instead a "Coalition
Executive Committee" was formed, with David Ben-Gurion as
chairman and Abba Hillel Silver as chairman of the American
section. Thus the leadership of the world movement now
passed into the hands of the Jews of Palestine themselves —
with the support of the all-important American community.

Two months later, in February, 1947, with the terror in
Palestine still unabated, British Foreign Secretary Ernest
Bevin arose in Parliament to announce that Britain would
now refer the entire Palestine problem to the United Nations.
His efforts to secure peace in the Near East had been thwarted,
Bevin said, by "certain New York Jews" — and President
Truman. The American President, never one to take an insult
quietly, denounced Bevin's speech as "false and misleading."
Bevin's uncalled-for attack was, in fact, a serious mistake.

A mistake because by 1947 (in fact, even earlier) it had
become painfully apparent to the entire world community
that the British Empire was in process of dissolution. The
British Labour Party had inherited, from the wartime coalition government of Winston Churchill, an empire victorious,
but bankrupt. This was a fact which few Britons, least of all
the Foreign Secretary, cared to face. The days were gone when
Britain's fleet ruled the seas, when word from London toppled
governments, when Britain was a Great Power in the full sense
of those words. Now she depended almost entirely upon American aid, both economic and military, for her very existence.
Her mighty war effort against Nazi Germany had bled her
white — and real power in the postwar world was divided between the United States and the Soviet Union. Furthermore,

the Second World War had unleashed powerful nationalistic impulses everywhere in the "colonial world." Throughout Africa and Asia, formerly subject peoples were throwing off the imperialistic shackles of Britain, France, and other colonial powers. It was a tide which Britain could not suppress — and the Jewish movement to "liberate" Palestine was but one wave of that tide. Nations, like people, are never so resentful as when they lose their "status." And this peculiar resentment may help to account for the petty nastiness and spleen with which Britain waged her battle against a Jewish Palestine from 1945 to 1948. As later years would show, this irrational behavior was only an unnatural aberration in British history; it did not reflect the real, permanent sentiments of the British people nor, for that matter, their true national interests.

Bevin's speech provoked a reaction in Palestine as well as in Washington. The Irgun attacked fifteen British police stations and blew up the British Officers' Club in Jerusalem. The British retaliated by imposing martial law and making more arrests, and by hanging four members of the Irgun on April 16, 1947. Six days later a British troop train was blown up.

Meantime, Arab guerrilla attacks against Jewish settlements and outbreaks of Arab mob fury in Jerusalem — all financed and instigated by the governments of neighboring Arab states — had never ceased, even during the war years. Since 1945 they had increased in number and ferocity, for as the Second World War drew to a close, Great Britain, sensing the difficulties ahead, sought to create a new instrument through which to control the Arab world in the Near East. This was the Arab League, created under British auspices in March, 1945. Egypt, Syria, Iraq, Lebanon, and Saudi Arabia were original members. Later, in 1946, when the British finally permitted the establishment of Transjordan as the fully independent state of Jordan (though still under British tutelage), it too joined the League. As for the Grand Mufti of Jerusalem — having fled the ruins of Nazi Germany, he was now alive and well in Cairo and doing his best to foment trouble in Palestine. The British (and some American State Department officials) thought the Arab League would stand as a buffer against Soviet Russian infiltration of the Near East; it could also be manipulated so as to insure the safety of the huge British-American investment in the oil industry of the region. How sadly mistaken they were only the future would reveal.

For the present, the Arab League immediately embarked on a really venomous anti-Jewish program. Throughout the Near East and North Africa, Jewish communities in Arab nations were subjected to bloody pogroms. This was but a foretaste of what would happen in Palestine should the Arabs prevail there.

On April 28, 1947, a special session of the United Nations Assembly opened in New York. It had been called to consider the question of Palestine. But could the Assembly agree? And if it could agree, could it act? Since World War II the division between the former wartime allies, the United States and Britain on one side, the Soviet Union and her satellites on the other, had deepened. Mutual suspicions had become mutual bitterness; the so-called Cold War between East and West had begun. Even if the United States and the Western democracies supported Jewish hopes in Palestine, would not the Soviet Union — where Zionism was considered high treason to the state — veto any progress?

This question was answered by Andrei Gromyko, the head of the Russian UN delegation on May 14, 1947. In a speech that took everyone by surprise, he told the UN General Assembly that both Jews and Arabs had "historical roots" in Palestine. Russia would prefer to see a binational Arab-Jewish state created there. But if "this plan was unrealizable . . . it would be necessary to consider an alternative solution . . . the division of Palestine into two independent states, one Jewish and one Arab." The Soviet Union now advocated what the Zionists had always wanted — a Jewish state in Palestine! Why this abrupt about-face in Soviet policy? The most probable reason was that the creation of a Jewish state in Palestine would put an end to British influence in that vitally strategic region so close to Russia's southern borders. In any event, suddenly — and for one of the few times in its history — the United Nations was able to deal with a problem without being bedeviled by Russian-American rivalry. The General Assembly voted to create a commission to investigate the problems in Palestine and report with recommendations the following November.

The UN commission listened to spokesmen for the Zionist cause, namely, Abba Hillel Silver, Moshe Sharett, and David Ben-Gurion. It also heard from representatives of the nations of the Arab League, and listened even to a representative of the Grand Mufti of Jerusalem (the Grand Mufti himself was wanted for war crimes and preferred to remain in Cairo). The Arabs stated that they would not cooperate with the committee in any way — and would fight any decision that led to the creation of a Jewish state in Palestine.

The UN committee, composed of representatives of eleven nations (the Great Powers were excluded) traveled extensively in Palestine. They spoke to Arabs and Jews. They interviewed leaders of the Haganah and even (at their secret headquarters) of the Irgun. They also visited the miserable Displaced Persons Camps in Europe where those Hundred Thousand still waited.

During the committee's sojourn in Palestine, the battle between Jews and the British authorities continued unabated. British counterterror activities were now entrusted to a special squad of British police which had been recruited from among the followers of Sir Oswald Mosley's vicious Union of British Fascists. Some of these men enjoyed the pastime of driving through the streets of Tel Aviv and firing into stores, cafes, and passing buses. One such attack cost the lives of five Jews and wounded twenty-seven others. On June 16, 1947, a British military court condemned to death three Jewish youths for having participated in an attack on the British prison at Acre, an attack which had resulted in the liberation of some two hundred fifty Jewish political prisoners. When the youths were executed in July, the Irgun retaliated by hanging two British soldiers. The Jewish press was unanimous in condemning this ruthless Irgun action.

Perhaps the saddest incident which occurred during the committee's investigation was the long travail of the coffin ship *Exodus 1947*. The ship, an old American coastal steamer built to carry 700 passengers, left a southern French fishing port on July 11, 1947, carrying 4,500 refugees, men, women, and children bound for Palestine, a tiny fraction of the Hundred Thousand, fleeing their nightmare past. A British squadron of one cruiser and three destroyers trailed the vessel across the Mediterranean for a week. On the night of July 21, with her lights out, the *Exodus* tried to elude her pursuers and make a dash for the shore of Palestine. But she was rammed by a British destroyer and then boarded by British marines. In the ensuing scuffle an American crewman and two refugees were killed, while a score were wounded. The ship was compelled to proceed, under British guard, to Haifa.

But now the British government inaugurated a new policy. Instead of transporting the *Exodus*'s passengers to the internment camps on Cyprus (which were overcrowded and, the British felt, too close to Palestine anyhow), it was decreed that these refugees would be transported back to their port of origin. So the passengers of *Exodus 1947* were crowded onto three British prison ships and taken to Marseilles. But how were the refugees to be landed? The French were willing to receive them — but only if they came willingly. And the refugees declared they would willingly land only in Palestine. For more than a month the British prison ships remained anchored in the harbor of Marseilles, their pitiful cargo suffering in cages above and below deck under the intense summer heat.

The resolution of the refugees did not break. They would not agree to debark in France. So the British decided on one final indignity. The three prison ships weighed anchor, sailed out into the Atlantic, and then proceeded to the German port city of Hamburg, in the British zone of occupation. There the refugees were carried bodily from their ships by British soldiers on September 8, 1947, and carted back to the former German concentration camps where so many of their friends and relatives had perished during the holocaust. And still their spirit did not break. When questioned about their nationality by British intelligence officers, they usually answered, "I am a Jew from Palestine and I want to go back to Palestine." "Then how did you ever become a victim of the Nazis in Europe?" would be the next question. "I was traveling," the reply.

Two thousand years of travel were, however, coming to an end. The UN Committee on Palestine submitted its report in October, 1947, advocating the creation of two separate states in Palestine, one Jewish, one Arab. In detail, the UN committee proposed that the Arabs (who numbered two thirds of the population and already owned about forty-six percent of the land) should largely retain what they owned — with certain minor adjustments. The Jews (who numbered about one third of the population but owned only six percent of the land) would be awarded the rest. That is to say, the UN com-

mittee was proposing the creation of a Jewish state out of
unowned and largely unoccupied lands. These lands were to
be found mostly in the arid Negev Desert. The city of Jerusalem and its immediate vicinity would be administered by a
UN commission which would protect its holy places for the
benefit of Jews, Arabs, and Christians alike. The solution
seemed reasonable. The Arabs would lose almost nothing, the
Jews would gain only what no one else apparently wanted. But
six weeks of furious debate by the General Assembly followed
this "reasonable" proposal.

In this debate the American delegation at first took a curi-
ously aloof and indifferent stand. The American State Department was not in agreement with either the White House or
the Congress on American Near East policy. Many State Department officials, taking their cue from the British, preferred
to play the oil-and-power game of appeasing the Arab states.

Once again American Zionists threw themselves into the
breach. They mustered all the influence, skill, and strength of
which they were capable. Leading Zionists, both Christian and
Jewish, made speeches; letters by the thousands poured in
upon congressmen; rallies were held throughout the country —
any and every means of persuasion available to free men in a
democratic society were used. And the State Department got
the message. Its support for the UN committee's report
changed from lukewarm to hot.

Finally, on November 29, 1947, the United Nations General
Assembly voted to accept their committee's plan. The vote was
33 in favor, 13 against, and 10 abstentions. All the Great Powers supported the plan except Great Britain, which abstained,
but every member of the British Commonwealth of Nations
voted in favor, defying London's policy. Jews throughout the
world rejoiced — at long last the political goal of the Zionist

movement had been achieved; the highest international authority, with the support of the Super-Powers, had decreed the creation of a Jewish state in Palestine.

But a decree was one thing, reality another. When the UN vote was announced, the delegates of the Arab nations walked out of the General Assembly. They would fight to the death against the UN plan, they announced. And Great Britain declared that although she would withdraw completely from Palestine within six months, she would do nothing to help implement the UN decision. In effect this meant that Britain would be siding with the Arabs — and that the battle between Jews and British forces in Palestine would go on.

The Arabs in Palestine responded to the UN vote by staging strikes, riots, and raids on Jewish settlements. As usual they were armed and led by Arabs from neighboring countries. The British, insisting that until they left they alone were responsible for maintaining order in the Holy Land, hampered Jewish defense forces by disarming them whenever they could, arresting their leaders, and continuing to deport "illegals" attempting to enter the country. On the other hand, it seemed that they made no serious effort to stop the infiltration of Arab guerrillas into Palestine from Egypt and Syria. Furthermore, the Arab armies which were now gathering to invade Palestine were armed, equipped, and, in the case of the Jordanian Legion, led by British officers. As British forces were withdrawn from certain sectors, the Jordanian Legion was brought in to take their place — with fatal consequences for many Jews. On December 15, for example, soldiers of the legion opened fire on a Jewish convoy of trucks near Lydda, killing 14 people and wounding 12.

During the five and one half months of guerrilla warfare between November, 1947, and May, 1948, more than 1,250 Jews were killed, as well as more than 3,500 Arabs and 152

British soldiers. Few of the dead Arabs were Palestinian. The so-called Arab Army of Liberation (led by a lieutenant of the Grand Mufti) was composed mostly of Arabs recruited in Syria, Iraq, and Egypt, and was supplied by these countries with British weapons.

A focal point of the fighting was the road which connected Jerusalem with Tel Aviv. The hundred thousand Jewish inhabitants of the New City, as well as the few thousand inhabitants of the Old City of Jerusalem, were always in danger of being cut off, for the road ran through Arab-controlled territory. The Haganah was badly prepared for battle. It was not yet an army — only an underground resistance force which could, at best, field some three thousand well-trained but badly equipped soldiers. Furthermore, whenever possible, the British imposed restraints on Haganah activity. Convoys carrying food, medicine and weapons from Tel Aviv to Jerusalem found themselves under incessant Arab guerrilla attack. Hundreds of Jews were killed and vehicles littered the sides of the road. A strong point along the route was the tiny village of Castel. This changed hands several times between the Haganah and Arab guerrillas before it was finally secured by the Jews on April 4, 1948. Only a few days later occurred an incident which filled the Jews with shame. On April 9 a group of Stern Gang members entered the Arab village of Deir Yassin and, when the inhabitants refused to surrender, killed 250 of them, including many women. This ruthless action was denounced by the Haganah, which now began the task of not only defending the Jewish community against Arab attack and British obstructionism, but also of capturing, disarming, and imprisoning Jewish extremists such as members of the Stern Gang whose methods could not be tolerated no matter how extreme the provocation.

On April 13 a convoy carrying much-needed food and medical supplies to the Hebrew University and the Hadassah Hospital on Mount Scopus outside Jerusalem was attacked and destroyed by Arab guerrillas. Most of the personnel accompanying this convoy — doctors and nurses, numbering seventy-six — were killed. The British prevented Haganah forces from going to the rescue of the convoy. Among the dead was Dr. Chaim Yassky, head of the Hadassah Medical Organization.

Not all the terrorism was Arab or Jewish. On February 1, the offices of the *Palestine Post* newspaper, and on March 11, a wing of the Jewish Agency headquarters were blown up by bombs. An inquiry revealed that British police had planted those bombs, which killed fifty-six people and wounded more than a hundred. In fact, credit for the bombings was claimed by an organization billing itself "The British Legion — Palestine Branch," in a pamphlet which declared: "We will finish Hitler's job."

The decisive battle of the guerrilla war was fought at the Jewish settlement of Mishmar Ha-Emek in April, 1948. The "Arab Army of Liberation" attacked this small village in force in an attempt to drive through to the sea, thereby splitting the Jewish area of Palestine in two. The Arab attackers outnumbered the defenders four to one; furthermore, they were much better armed, having not only automatic weapons, but even tanks. Yet the defenders of Mishmar Ha-Emek held out until, on April 15, the Haganah arrived to help them. The Arabs were routed.

By the middle of April, as the British withdrew from various areas of Palestine preparatory to their final departure (which, in compliance with the UN resolution, London had set for May 15), a strange phenomenon began to occur. The Arab masses in various cities, and in the countryside, too, began fleeing from their homes. Their flight was not due to panic alone, or to Jewish military action. It was largely brought about by directives from Arab leaders outside Palestine — and the flight was assisted by the British. Palestinian Arabs were told that the armies of Egypt, Syria, Iraq, and Jordan would invade Palestine as soon as the British departed. It would be better for them to get out completely to avoid being caught up in the coming battles. Then, after the Jews had been massacred or thrown into the sea, the Palestinians could return. They would be away only a short time, since victory would come rapidly.

Thus when, on April 19, the Haganah captured Tiberius from Arab guerrillas, the native Arab population fled. Three days later, when the Haganah captured Haifa, almost all of its seventy thousand Arab inhabitants departed — despite the Haganah's invitation to them to stay. The story was the same at Safed, that ancient home of Jewish dreamers and scholars. Everywhere throughout Palestine the Arabs were fleeing over the borders. The most spectacular flight of all occurred at Jaffa. That city, with its hundred thousand Arab citizens, was not even to be included in the new Jewish state. The Jews had no interest in the place except for the fact that Arab guerrillas used it as a base for attacks on neighboring Tel Aviv. When a Haganah detachment attempted to put an end to these Arab forays, the British intervened, placing their military forces between Jaffa and Tel Aviv. But when the British left Jaffa, on May 12, 1948 — despite the fact that no Jewish forces had ever reached the city and also despite the fact that the Jews had specifically announced that they had no intention of incorporating Jaffa into their new nation — the entire Arab population of the place fled. The Haganah entered a deserted city.

It was in these tragic circumstances that the Arab refugee problem was born. Palestinian refugees were later to claim that they had been driven from their homeland by the Jews; Israelis were to claim that most had been lured or frightened away by the promises and threats of the Arab leaders both inside and outside Palestine. But certain facts remain indisputable. In 1947 there were some 1,200,000 Arabs living in all of Palestine. Of this number about 1,000,000 lived *outside* the borders of the proposed Jewish state — in areas into which, during their War of Independence, the Jews *never penetrated*. Of those 200,000 Arabs who lived within the area awarded to the Jews by the United Nations, an indeterminate number (which may have been as high as 100,000) fled. Of these, a very large proportion returned when hostilities died down. Nor must it be forgotten that more than 350,000 Arabs live today in the state of Israel (*not* including those living in regions conquered since 1948) as Israeli citizens — enjoying, incidentally, a standard of living four times higher than that enjoyed by Arabs in neighboring states. If the Jews had been determined to drive the Arabs from their new nation, how is it that they failed so miserably? The facts do not support the claims of Arab leaders. The facts would seem to indicate that the Arab refugee problem was, at least in large part, created by those leaders themselves — first because they wanted a clear field for their armies to destroy the Jews, and later prolonged, as we shall see, for political reasons.

As the British left Palestine, during the last two weeks of April and the beginning of May, 1948, they seemed determined to destroy everything that had been built up during the past three decades. Palestinian assets in England, amounting to some £100,000,000, were frozen; the oil refineries at Haifa were closed down; all imports were suspended; railway traffic was halted; postal and telegraphic services were ended; Lydda airport was closed so that international air traffic came to a halt; dispensable British army supplies and vehicles were sold to the Arabs, and British barracks and military camps turned over to Arab guerrillas. The Jews were not permitted to run any of these essential services themselves, nor was the United Nations Commission on Palestine allowed to intervene. The British refused the commission's request to open a port for Jewish immigration, and they refused to allow the formation of Jewish and Arab police forces to maintain order in their respective zones. They seemed determined to leave nothing but chaos behind.

The British Mandate was to end on May 15, 1948. And on that same date, promised the Arab leaders, their armies would invade Palestine and crush the Jews. The armed forces of Syria, Egypt, and Iraq were poised on the borders, ready to deliver a death blow; the Jordanian Legion, thanks to the British, already occupied strategic positions within Palestine. The Egyptian air force was prepared to bomb Tel Aviv, Jerusalem, and other ta gets — and the Haganah had no planes with which to defend or retaliate against such attacks. In fact, although the Haganah had been well able to handle the guerrilla war, it lacked the tanks, artillery, and weapons to withstand this impending full-scale invasion. Nor was there any place into which the Jews of Palestine could retreat. In light of all this, what was the life expectancy of a Jewish state? But then, the odds had always been impossible. . . .

They had been impossible for Bar Kochba nearly two thousand years earlier when the Romans savagely extinguished the last Jewish Commonwealth; they had been impossible during all the long centuries of dispersion and bitter persecution. They had seemed impossible fifty-three years earlier, in 1895, when Herzl had written in his *Judenstaat:* "The Jews who will it shall have a state of their own." Few paid any attention then to the Austrian dreamer; few paid any attention later when the First Zionist World Congress met at Basel. But much had happened since then; two World Wars, depressions both great and small, promises made and promises broken, the dreadful horror of the holocaust, and now at last with the odds still impossible . . .

At four o'clock in the afternoon of May 14, 1948, the members of the provisional national council, led by David Ben-Gurion, met in the Tel Aviv Art Museum. A few hours before, the British High Commissioner and the last group of British officials had left for England. One last promise, that of the mandate, had finally been broken. Now David Ben-Gurion rose and read to the assembled council members and some fifty distinguished guests a proclamation:

"The Land of Israel was the birthplace of the Jewish people. Here their spiritual, religious and national identity was formed. Here they achieved independence and created a culture of national and universal significance. Here they wrote and gave the Bible to the world.

"Exiled from Palestine, the Jewish people remained faithful to it in all countries of their dispersion, never ceasing to pray and hope for their return and the restoration of their national freedom. . . .

"Accordingly we, the members of the National Council, representing the Jewish people in Palestine and the Zionist movement of the world, met together in solemn assembly today, the day of termination of the British Mandate for Palestine, by virtue of the natural and historic right of the Jewish people and the Resolution of the General Assembly of the United Nations, hereby proclaim the establishment of the Jewish state in Palestine, to be called ISRAEL. . . .

"With trust in Almighty God, we set our hand to this Declaration, at this session of the Provisional State Council, in the city of Tel Aviv, on this Sabbath eve, the fifth of Iyar, 5708, the fourteenth day of May, 1948."

Many of the assembly wept. They sang "Hatikvah" and listened to the ancient benediction: "Blessed art Thou, O Lord our God, King of the Universe, who has kept us in life, and preserved us and enabled us to reach this season." A journalist in beleaguered Jerusalem, Harry Levin, wrote that day: "So the lamp snuffed out nearly 2,000 years ago was relighted today. A miracle as great as any that ever happened in this land . . ."

Another "miracle" occurred in far-off Washington, D.C. Within ten minutes of Ben-Gurion's proclamation in Tel Aviv came the best birthday present for which the infant state could have hoped: the President of the United States, Harry S Truman, extended official recognition to both the new nation and its government. This meant that Israel could purchase arms and supplies from America with which to defend itself; it meant that America's many client states in South America and throughout the world would now follow suit; it meant the political, economic, and moral support of the most powerful nation on earth. This instant American recognition was the crowning victory of the American Zionist movement; but it would have been impossible had not the terrible sufferings of the Jews of Europe and the gallant struggle of the Jews of Palestine struck a responsive chord in the American national conscience.

So Israel was reborn, and the miracle came to pass. But what Zionism had wrought, Zionism had now to preserve. For one minute after midnight on May 15, 1948, the Arab forces struck. The Egyptian air force bombed Tel Aviv and the Egyptian army drove deep into the Negev. The next day the armies of Syria, Lebanon, and Jordan, supported by contingents from Saudi Arabia and Iraq, also invaded Israel. Abdul Rahman Azzam Pasha, the Secretary General of the Arab League, declared: "This will be a war of extermination and a momentous massacre, which will be spoken of like the Mongol massacres and the Crusades." This seemed no idle boast. The well-equipped armies of nations with a combined population of some 40,000,000 people were attacking the ill-equipped defense forces of a nation of 650,000.

Israel's War of Independence lasted some eight months. It was fought not only on the battlefields of Palestine but in the capitals and great cities of the world as well. For now the World Zionist movement went into high gear. Rifles and automatic weapons were bought (mostly from Czechoslovakia), old tanks and artillery were purchased from South and Central American nations, war-surplus planes were obtained from the United States — weapons, ammunition, and supplies were gathered wherever and by whatever means necessary from all over the world and rushed to Israel. A call for volunteers brought surprising responses in the United States, France, Canada, England, and other countries. Without this support it is doubtful that the *Zva Haganah le-Israel*, the "Defense Army of Israel" (as the Haganah emerging from underground now called itself), would have been able to repel the invaders. But repel them they did, after a bitter struggle — even driving them in defeat beyond the borders of the new state. There were several truces, during which the United Nations attempted to arbitrate between the Arab states and Israel, but these uneasy cease-fires were never respected by the Arab armies. Only when, in October, 1948, the Israeli army went on the offensive and, in a brilliant seven-day campaign called "Operation Ten Plagues," utterly routed the Egyptian forces and even invaded Egypt itself, did the Arabs agree to an armistice. The "peace" which followed was in no way real — but it was the best that Israel could hope for at the time.

In his diary, fifty years earlier, Herzl had written: "God breaks the instruments that have served His purpose." Zionism, it would seem, had been such an instrument. With the state of Israel established and preserved, and its admission into the United Nations on May 11, 1949, it might well appear that the Zionist movement had served its purpose and could now come to an end. But history rarely provides either clear-cut beginnings or endings; instead, it provides problems. Zionism today, in the third decade of the Third Jewish Commonwealth, remains such a problem.

Epilogue:

A Problem of Survival . . .

To many people throughout the world, including some Jews, it seemed that the Zionist mission was completed on May 14, 1948. After all, Zionists themselves had set their goal at the First World Zionist Congress in Basel in 1897 as the restoration of a Jewish state in Palestine. With Israel a vibrant reality just fifty years later, it appeared that the Zionist movement could now retire as a force in world affairs. But, just as Zionism did not start with Theodor Herzl and his World Zionist Congress, it did not end with the establishment of the state of Israel.

It did not end, in the first place, because it still found urgent and practical tasks. When one such task was completed, another would arise, and then another. For example, when the Israeli War of Independence ended and a permanent government was established (Chaim Weizmann was elected Israel's first president, David Ben-Gurion its first prime minister), Zionists faced the immense task of organizing and financing the "ingathering" — the return of homeless or persecuted Jews to their new homeland. This was a problem beyond the capacities of the infant nation to perform alone. During the first three years of its existence Israel welcomed home more than six hundred thousand Jews — with funds mostly provided by the American Zionist Organization. These Jews came from the internment camps of Cyprus and Mauritius, from the Displaced Persons Camps of Europe. They came from Poland, where, beginning in 1946, a vicious wave of anti-Semitic outrages arose against the survivors of the holocaust; they came from Bulgaria, Yugoslavia, and other eastern European countries where newly installed Communist regimes sought to stamp out Jewish identity. They came, too, from the Islamic world, where news of Israeli independence touched off pogroms against Jewish communities in Morocco, Algeria, Tunisia, and elsewhere. The ancient Jewish community of Yemen, for example, was airlifted to Israel in "Operation Magic Carpet," that of Iraq was saved through "Operation Ali Baba." Neither of these rescue missions could have been undertaken without the organizational and financial support of the World Zionist Organization.

Then, when the most urgent rescue missions of the ingathering had been completed, a second task emerged: to help establish the new state on a sound economic basis. To absorb so many refugees so soon (and they kept coming over the years) was beyond the resources of Israel. But through such Zionist organs as the United Jewish Appeal and the Christian Palestine Committee, the money, the machine tools, the seeds, and the factories were, in large part, provided. Within a decade of its founding, Israel had developed a full-fledged and prosperous national economy.

Of course, much remained to accomplish. In a land where everything had to be created there were hardships, shortages, and economic crises. But the new state was buoyant with economic self-confidence and, in the zest of building a nation, privations seemed bearable. Israel became a good investment and supportive American Zionists (Christian as well as Jewish) backed their sentiments with cash. When, in the spring of 1951, Prime Minister Ben-Gurion toured the United States (as a guest of the American Zionist Organization) to launch a drive for the sale of Israeli government bonds, more than $500,000,000 worth were sold in a matter of weeks. Such Israeli bond drives have been a recurring feature of American life ever since — they were and are organized by the various committees and branches of the American Zionist movement.

But once the ingathering had been completed, once the state of Israel had achieved a relatively secure economy, what tasks remained for the Zionist movement? There was one — the most vital task of all — that of defending the nation's very existence. It was a task unsought by Zionists but imposed upon them by Israel's Arab neighbors, for the Arab states ringing Israel's borders had never accepted the decision of the War of Independence. Egypt, Syria, Jordan, with the active support of the entire Near Eastern Arab world, vowed to exterminate the new nation. As a result, since 1948 Israel has had to fight three "wars" against her Arab neighbors: the Suez War of 1956, the Six-Day War of 1967, and the Yom Kippur War of 1973. But in actuality, these "wars" have been no more than campaigns in an ongoing war which began in 1948 (some might say 1921) and has continued to this day. There has never been a moment of real peace during this war; in the intervals between large-scale military operations, Israelis have had to fight a never-ending battle against Arab terrorists and guerrillas. Israel's ability to defend itself militarily has been triumphantly demonstrated again and again over the years. But wars do not have to be military; they can also be political, and on the political war front, the worldwide Zionist movement has provided indispensable help.

If Israel's armed forces have been supplied and resupplied

with American weapons; if every American President since Harry Truman has solemnly pledged that the United States will never permit Israel to be destroyed — these political victories have been won, in large part, by the untiring efforts of American Zionists. Again and again it has been necessary to mobilize American public opinion, to lobby in Congress, to organize ad hoc and emergency committees — in short to use all the many processes of American democracy to ensure continuing American support for Israel. Without the dedicated work of various American Zionist leaders and organizations, it is uncertain whether American support for Israel would have been so unswerving. But in gaining that support American Zionists have had to answer difficult questions.

First of all, there were those who said that Zionism after 1948 was no more than a tool of Israeli foreign policy. Furthermore, it was claimed that Israeli foreign policy did not necessarily coincide with the best interests of the United States. The first part of this allegation was simplistic, but essentially true. With the establishment of the state of Israel, the relationship between that state and the Zionist movement throughout the world underwent significant changes. No longer could Zionists in Britain, France, or (more importantly) America impose their views upon the Jews of Palestine. After all, the new Jewish state knew its own needs better than anyone else. So now it was Israelis who advised Zionists elsewhere on how best they could help. While this by no means meant that Zionists took dictation from the Israeli government, it did mean that Zionists, in their role of worldwide defenders of the Jewish state, generally (but not always) accepted the Israeli government's view of how that defense should be conducted. In a sense, then, the history of Zionism after 1948 merges into the history of the state of Israel — a subject beyond the scope of this book.

Of all the Israeli policies with which Zionism has identified itself since 1948, the most difficult for Zionists to justify to the world has centered around the problem of the Palestinian Arab refugees. These were the survivors of the Arab flight from Palestine in 1948 and their descendants. Whether they were frightened from their homes by Israeli military actions or lured from them by the promises of Arab leaders was not really the point. The point was that they existed and by 1977 numbered more than half a million — half a million stateless people living, for the most part, in abysmal refugee camps and villages in Syria, Lebanon, Egypt, and Jordan, where they were supported by world charity and where they nursed a deep and bitter hatred of Israel. Armed and trained by their "hosts," the Palestinian refugees have carried on an endless war of terror not only against the Jews of Israel but against Jews throughout the world and against Christians they perceive as supporting the Israeli cause. They have developed a heightened political awareness over the years since 1948 and have created such military-political instruments as the Palestine Liberation Organization (PLO) to organize and lead their struggle. Until the problem of what to do with these stateless people is solved, there can be no peace in the Near East.

There were always three possible solutions to this question. The Arab refugees could be absorbed into the Arab world — become citizens of the countries in which they found refuge — they could be readmitted into Israel; they could be given a new state of their own. But each solution presented great difficulties.

The Arab nations ringing Israel have not wished to absorb the Palestinian refugees for various reasons. At first, and for many years, Arab leaders in those nations preferred to segregate the Palestinian refugees in their squalid camps and villages as propaganda pawns to play on the conscience of the world; later their continuing misery served to recruit them for the ceaseless guerrilla war waged against Israel. Still later, Arab governments saw the Palestinian refugees, now armed, organized, and bloodied in combat, as a threat to their own internal security; in Jordan, Syria, and Lebanon, Arab rulers have waged bloody campaigns against the Palestinians in an effort to suppress them. In any event, irrespective of the views of Arab governments, the Palestinians themselves do not wish to be "absorbed" into their host countries. They demand the right to return to their homeland, Palestine — which brings us to the second possible solution.

The Palestine from which the Arab refugees fled in 1948 no longer exists. It is now occupied by the state of Israel. The lands on which the refugees once dwelt are owned by Israelis; their homes have, for the most part, given way to Israeli farms, suburbs, and cities. To what life then, could they return? The Israeli government, pointing out the fact that for thirty years the Palestinian refugees have been propagandized, armed, and trained for war and terrorist activities against Jews, declares that to admit them back into Israel would be to admit a vicious and dangerous fifth column into the land. The Palestinians themselves, through the leader of the PLO, Yasir Arafat, declare that they wish to see Palestine converted into a secular (that is, nonreligious) state in which both Arabs and Jews would live on terms of equality. Although Israel is not a "religious" state, it is definitely a nation governed by Jewish tradition, customs, and observances. And while freedom of religion is both guaranteed and freely practiced in Israel (nearly four hundred thousand Moslems live there as citizens), Judaism, which, as we have seen, is inseparable from Jewish national identity, is the officially recognized state religion. To convert Israel into a "secular" state would be to destroy it as a Jewish nation. This the Israelis will never accept. But, of

course, the state of Israel does not comprise all of what was
once Palestine — which brings us to the third possible solution.

Various Arab and American leaders have proposed that the
Palestinian refugees be granted a state of their own in those
parts of Palestine which were not originally Israeli territory —
the Gaza Strip and the West Bank of the River Jordan. These
regions were conquered by the Israelis during the Six-Day War
of 1963 and are still occupied by them. As part of a general
peace settlement in the Near East it has been suggested that
the Israelis withdraw from these conquered lands, which
would then comprise a new Palestinian refugee state. Arafat
and other Palestinian leaders have indicated that, while not re-
nouncing their ultimate goal of destroying Israel, they might
accept this solution. King Hussein of Jordan (from whose pre-
1963 domains the West Bank area would be carved) has indicated his reluctant agreement. But the Israeli government currently opposes such a solution. They point out that the West
Bank area, lacking sufficient land, resources, and cities, cannot
constitute any kind of economically viable state. The new nation, they fear, would simply be one vast Displaced Persons
Camp, to be supported by world charity. Furthermore, it
would constitute a huge base of operations for Arab terrorists
right on Israel's border.

Threading their way through all these conflicts and arguments, Zionists throughout the world have been guided by two
basic convictions: first, that Israel must and shall survive as a
Jewish state; second, that Israelis best understand Israel's
needs. Therefore Zionists in America and elsewhere have consistently supported Israeli policies in the Near East even when
the governments of their own countries have not. Arab leaders
have seized upon this fact as "proof" that Zionists place al-

legiance to their "Jewish race" above all other loyalties. This, they claim, makes Zionism a form of racism.

Of course the Arab leaders themselves (most of whom are educated, sophisticated, and well-traveled) know perfectly well that this accusation is untrue. But it makes persuasive propaganda in their own (and other) countries where freedom and democracy are unknown. For the uneducated, oppressed masses throughout much of the world simply cannot imagine a free, pluralistic, open society like that of the United States — a society in which people of many different ethnic backgrounds may be loyal to different religious, national, or cultural heritages while remaining patriotic Americans.

And so the Arab leaders, eager to win a propaganda victory over Israel, cynically brought forward at the United Nations General Assembly the charge that Zionism is a form of racism. There they won support from Communist and many Third World nations who were eager to win a propaganda victory over the United States and other democratic countries who support Israel. And since Arab, Communist, and Third World dictatorships far outnumber democracies in that august chamber, they were able to win the vote of November 10, 1975.

They were able to win the vote — but they were unable to persuade free and reasonable people anywhere of the truth of their accusation. In fact, their propaganda victory served only to enrage the literate portion of mankind, who recalled that Jews, for more than two thousand years, have been the world's most abject victims of racism. But rejecting the Arab-Communist definition of Zionism brings us back to the problem of history with which this book began: what is Zionism?

It depends on your viewpoint. If you are a Palestinian refugee you may well see Zionism as a worldwide conspiracy which has robbed you of your homeland. If you are a Communist you will see it as merely another arm of American "imperialist foreign policy" — a means of exploiting, through the state of Israel, the resources of the Near East. If you have no particular ideological axe to grind you will probably see it as the means whereby the Jews regained and preserved their ancient homeland. Can it be defined, from any viewpoint at all, as racism? Racism, in its broad (and most widely accepted) sense, is the belief that humankind can be categorized according to "race" — with the very clear implication that there are superior races (one's own) and inferior races (everyone else's). Such beliefs have led, inexorably, to genocide — the murder of entire peoples by those who considered themselves of "superior race." There are many examples of genocide: the wiping out of the North American Indians, the recent mass murder of the Ibo tribes in Nigeria, the fate of aboriginal populations in Australia and elsewhere. But of course the greatest example of all was the Nazi genocide that consumed more than six million Jews during the holocaust. As Jews, Zionists throughout history have had to wage a never-ending battle against racism. Nowhere in Zionist teaching, philosophy, or action can the faintest taint of racism be found. Racism is diametrically opposed to all Jewish belief and practice. To impute to Jews the very evil from which they have suffered so terribly throughout history is a truly vicious, truly ignorant slander.

Zionism, then, can only be defined as a historical movement — but not one which commenced with Theodor Herzl, for in a deeper and truer sense Zionism has been the meaning of Jewish history and belief from its very beginnings. Abraham was a Zionist when he abandoned Ur of the Chaldees to seek a promised land; Moses was a Zionist who led his people out of bondage and back to the hills of Zion; the Prophets of the Babylonian Exile were Zionists who never gave up the dream of the Return. So too were those millions of Jews who suffered through the long night of the Diaspora, awaiting a dawn that was to be delayed for nearly two thousand years. The very ancient toast always offered by Jews throughout the world on Passover, "Next year in Jerusalem," expresses a Zionism so deeply imbedded in Jewish culture and religion as to be inextinguishable. For to Jews, Zionism in its deepest and oldest meaning is nothing less than obedience to God's will — and the love of that tiny piece of creation He willed to the descendants of Abraham.

Bibliography

Abbott, George F., *Israel in Europe*. New York: Macmillan (1907).

Addelson, G. F., *Epic of a People*. New York: Bloch (1943).

Anderson, Bernard W., *Understanding the Old Testament*. Englewood Cliffs: Prentice-Hall (1966).

Ben-Gurion, David, *Ben-Gurion Looks Back*. New York: Simon and Schuster (1965).

—— *The Jews in Their Land*. Garden City: Doubleday (1966).

Bodenheimer, Max I., *Prelude to Israel*. New York: T. Yoseloff (1963).

Borchsenius, R. F., *History of the Jews*, 5 vols. New York: Simon and Schuster (1965).

Brandeis, Louis D., *Brandeis on Zionism*. Washington, D.C.: Zionist Organization of America (1947).

Cohen, Israel, *The Zionist Movement*. New York: Zionist Organization of America (1946).

Crossman, Richard H. S., *Palestine Mission*. New York: Harper & Row (1947).

De Haas, Jacob, *Louis D. Brandeis*. New York: Bloch (1929).

Dimont, Max I., *Jews, God and History*. New York: Simon and Schuster (1962).

Dinin, Samuel, *Zionist Education in the United States*. Philadelphia: Zionist Organization of America (1944).

Eban, Abba S., *My People*. New York: Behrman House (1968).

Fast, Howard M., *The Jews*. New York: Dial Press (1968).

Friedlander, Albert H., *Out of the Whirlwind*. New York: Doubleday (1968).

228   BIBLIOGRAPHY

Feinstein, Marnin, *American Zionism*. New York: Herzl Press (1965).

Goldberg, Israel, *Fulfillment*. Cleveland: World (1951).

Goldman, Guido G., *Zionism under Soviet Rule*. New York: Herzl Press (1960).

Gonen, Jay Y., *A Psychohistory of Zionism*. New York: Mason/Charter (1975).

Grayzel, Solomon, *History of the Jews*. Philadelphia: Jewish Publication Society (1959).

Halpern, Ben, *The Idea of the Jewish State*. Cambridge, Mass.: Harvard University Press (1961).

Hertzberger, Arthur, *The Zionist Idea*. New York: Doubleday (1959).

Herzl, Theodore, *Diaries*, ed. and trans. Marvin Lowenthal. New York: Dial Press (1956).

——— *The Jewish State*, trans. Sylvie D'Avigdor. London: Zionist Organization (1936).

Josephus, Flavius, *Complete Works*, trans. William Whiston. New York: World (1821).

Keller, Werner, *Diaspora*. New York: Harcourt-Brace-Jovanovich (1969).

Kurland, Samuel, *Biluim: Pioneers in Palestine*. New York: Scopus (1943).

Laqueur, Walter Z., *A History of Zionism*. New York: Holt, Rinehart and Winston (1977).

Lehman, Emil, *Israel: Idea and Reality*. New York: United Synagogue Commission on Jewish Education (1962).

Litvinoff, Barnet, *To the House of Their Fathers*. New York: Praeger (1965).

Main, Ernest, *Palestine at the Crossroads*. London: Allen & Unwin (1939).

Margolis, Max L., *History of the Jewish People*. Philadelphia: Jewish Publication Society of America (1927).

Miller, Irving, *Israel: The Eternal Ideal*. New York: Farrar, Strauss (1955).

Naiditch, Isaac, *Edmond de Rothschild*. Washington, D.C.: Zionist Organization of America (1945).

Nardi, Noach, *Education in Palestine*. Washington, D.C.: Zionist Organization of America (1945).

Patai, Raphael (ed.), *Encyclopedia of Zionism*. New York: Herzl Press (1971).

Polk, William R., *Backdrop to Tragedy*. Boston: Beacon Press (1957).

Radin, Max, *The Jews among the Greeks and Romans*. Philadelphia: Jewish Publication Society (1915).

Revusky, Abraham, *The Jews in Palestine*. New York: Vanguard Press (1945).

Rose, N. A., *The Gentile Zionists*. London: Frank Cass (1973).

Rosenberg, Jehiel M., *The Story of Zionism*. New York: Bloch (1946).

Ruppin, Arthur, *Building Israel*. New York: Schocken Books (1949).

Sanders, Ronald, *Israel: The View from Masada*. New York: Harper Bros. (1966).

Sankowsky, Shohanna, *A Short History of Zionism*. New York: Bloch (1947).

Savage, Raymond, *Allenby of Armageddon*. Indianapolis: Bobbs-Merrill (1926).

Silver, Abba Hillel, *Vision and Victory*. New York: Zionist Organization of America (1949).

Sokolow, Nahum, *History of Zionism*. London: Longmans, Green (1919).

Suhl, Yuri, *They Fought Back*. New York: Crown (1967).

Sykes, Christopher, *Crossroads to Israel*. Cleveland: World (1965).

Thompson, Dorothy, *Let the Promise Be Fulfilled*. New York: American Christian Palestine Committee (1946).

Tuchman, Barbara W., *Bible and Sword*. New York: Funk & Wagnalls (1968).

Van Paassen, Pierre, *The Forgotten Ally*. New York: Dial Press (1943).

Weizmann, Chaim, *Autobiography of Chaim Weizmann*. New York: Harper & Row (1949).

Wise, Stephen S., *As I See It*. New York: Jewish Opinion Publishers (1944).

Zhabotinskii, Vladimir E., *The War and the Jews*. New York: Dial Press (1942).

Suggested Reading

For the ancient history of the Jews nothing can compare to reading the Holy Bible (preferably the King James version) for yourself. Read, too, *Understanding the Old Testament* by Bernard W. Anderson and, on the Jewish revolt against Rome, *The Complete Works of Flavius Josephus.*

Of the very many histories of the Jews available which deal with the Diaspora, R. F. Borchsenius's *History of the Jews* in five volumes is masterful and recent, but Howard Fast's *The Jews* is easier reading; so too is *Fulfillment,* by Israel Goldberg.

Books dealing specifically with Zionism are many. *Fulfillment,* mentioned above, is a good basic text, while Walter Laqueur's *History of Zionism,* recently reissued, is definitive. See too, Ronald Sanders's *Israel: The View from Masada* and Ben Halpern's *The Idea of the Jewish State* for the philosophy of Zionism. Herzl's *Diaries,* Chaim Weizmann's *Autobiography,* David Ben-Gurion's *Ben-Gurion Looks Back* all tell the story of the great Zionist leaders.

Index

hoped for by, 144, 155; World Zionist Congress of, 216; Zionism and, 224

Hess, Moses, 102–103; *Rome and Jerusalem, the Latest National Question*, 103

Hirsch, Baron Maurice de, 115

Hirsch family, 116, 119

Histadrut. *See* General Federation of Hebrew Workers in Israel

Hitler, Adolf, 182, 208; *Mein Kampf (My Battle)*, 160; his insane hatred of Jews, 160, 175; coming to power of, 165; and Arab Revolt (1936), 167, 168; conquest of Poland by, 174; extermination of German, Polish, and Russian Jews by, 175–176; extermination campaign of, 176–178; death of, 190

Holland, 77, 81, 83

"Hope, The." *See* "Hatikvah"

Horvitch, Harris and Bernard, 131

Hoshea, 16

Hundred Thousand, 190, 194–196, 198, 202, 203

Hussein, King, 222

Husseini, Amin El (Grand Mufti of Jerusalem), 152, 154, 182, 201, 202; and Arab Revolt (1936), 167–168

Ibn Albalia, Isaac, 38

Ibn Nagrela, Samuel, 38

Ibn Yaish, Solomon, 60, 61

Ikhnaton, Pharaoh, 9

Imber, Naphtali Herz, 117

Immigration, battle of, between Britain and Zionism, 186–191, 197

Ingathering, 216–217, 218

International Ladies Garment Workers Union, 101

Irgun Zvai Leumi (National Military Organization), 188–189; acts of terrorism by, against British, 196–197, 199, 203; UN interviews with, 202

Isaac, 6, 8

Isabella of Castile, 52–53

Islam: beginning of history of, 35–40; Palestine subject to, 55

Israel, 216; meaning of word, 6; kingdom of, 15, 16; Ben-Gurion's proclamation establishing, 212; American recognition of, 213; and War of Independence, 213–214; admission of, to UN, 214–215; development of prosperous economy in, 217; sale of government bonds for, 218; and problem of Palestinian Arab refugees, 220–222. *See also* Palestine

Israeli Air Force, 125

Israelites, 7–12

Israels, Jozef, 89

Isserles, Moses, 65

Italy: status of Jews in, after Protestant Reformation, 78; emancipation of Jews in, 81, 84; anti-Jewish regulations reimposed in, 83; and WW I, 143

Jacob, 6, 7, 8

Jacobi, Moritz, 88

Jacobs, Rose, 132

Jaffa, 209

Jastrow, Morris, 131, 132

Jemal Pasha, 137–138

Jerusalem: conquered by David, 15; return of exiled Jews to, 18; rebuilding of, as Roman City, 25, 26; Judah ha-Levi's death in, 55; Jewish community established in, 60, 106; Theodor Herzl on, 120; fall of, 145, 146–147; New City of, 166

Jesus of Nazareth, 24, 32, 33

Jew, derivation of word, 17

Jewish Agency, 158, 160–161, 164; lives saved by, in WW II, 179; British outlawing of, 196; headquarters of, blown up by British, 208

Jewish Colonial Trust, 129–130, 135

Jewish Committee, 149

Jewish Legion, 145

Jewish National Fund, 135

"Jewish Question," 88, 90, 102, 112, 113

Jewish Self-Defense Forces. *See* Haganah

Johann ben Zakkai, 29–30

Jonathan (Alexander Jannaeus), 21–22

Jordanian Legion, 206, 211

Joseph, 7

Joseph II of Austria, Emperor, 79–80